JAN -- 2004

Student Companion to
Richard
WRIGHT

Student Companion to

Richard
WRIGHT

Robert Felgar

Student Companions to Classic Writers

Greenwood Press
Westport, Connecticut • London

Library of Congress Cataloging-in-Publication Data

Felgar, Robert, 1944–
    Student companion to Richard Wright / Robert Felgar.
        p.   cm.—(Student companions to classic writers, ISSN 1522-7979)
    Includes bibliographical references (p.   ) and index.
    ISBN 0–313–30909–4 (alk. paper)
    1. Wright, Richard, 1908–1960—Criticism and interpretation.   2. Afro-Americans in
    literature.   I. Title.   II. Series.
    PS3545.R815 Z65175   2000
    813'.52—dc21   99–055115

British Library Cataloguing in Publication Data is available.

Library of Congress Catalog Card Number: 99–055115
ISBN: 0–313–30909–4
ISSN: 1522–7979

First published in 2000

Greenwood Press, 88 Post Road West, Westport, CT 06881
An imprint of Greenwood Publishing Group, Inc.
www.greenwood.com

Printed in the United States of America

(∞)™

The paper used in this book complies with the
Permanent Paper Standard issued by the National
Information Standards Organization (Z39.48–1984).

10 9 8 7 6 5 4 3 2

Contents

To Griffin and Noah

Series Foreword

This series has been designed to meet the needs of students and general readers for accessible literary criticism on the American and world writers most frequently studied and read in the secondary school, community college, and four-year college classrooms. Unlike other works of literary criticism that are written for the specialist and graduate student, or that feature a variety of reprinted scholarly essays on sometimes obscure aspects of the writer's work, the Student Companions to Classic Writers series is carefully crafted to examine each writer's major works fully and in a systematic way, at the level of the nonspecialist and general reader. The objective is to enable the reader to gain a deeper understanding of the work and to apply critical thinking skills to the act of reading. The proven format for the volumes in this series was developed by an advisory board of teachers and librarians for a successful series published by Greenwood Press, Critical Companions to Popular Contemporary Writers. Responding to their request for easy-to-use and yet challenging literary criticism for students and adult library patrons, Greenwood Press developed a systematic format that is not intimidating but helps the reader to develop the ability to analyze literature.

How does this work? Each volume in the Student Companions to Classic Writers series is written by a subject specialist, an academic who understands students' needs for basic and yet challenging examination of the writer's canon. Each volume begins with a biographical chapter, drawn from published sources, biographies, and autobiographies, that relates the writer's life to his or her work. The next chapter examines the writer's literary heritage, tracing the literary influences of other writers on that writer and explaining and discussing the literary genres into which the writer's work falls. Each of the following chapters examines a major work by the writer, those works most frequently read and studied by high school and college students. Depending on the writer's canon, generally between four and eight major works are examined, each in an individual chapter. The discussion of each work is organized into separate sections on plot development, character development, and major themes. Literary devices and style, narrative point of view, and historical setting are also discussed in turn if pertinent to the work. Each chapter concludes with an alternate critical perspective from which to read the work, such as a psychological or feminist criticism. The critical theory is defined briefly in easy, comprehensible language for the student. Looking at the literature from the point of view of a particular critical approach will help the reader to understand and apply critical theory to the act of reading and analyzing literature.

Of particular value in each volume is the bibliography, which includes a complete bibliography of the writer's works, a selected bibliography of biographical and critical works suitable for students, and lists of reviews of each work examined in the companion, all of which will be helpful to readers, teachers, and librarians who would like to consult additional sources.

As a source of literary criticism for the student or for the general reader, this series will help the reader to gain understanding of the writer's work and skill in critical reading.

1

The Life of
Richard Wright

One of the preeminent U.S. writers of the twentieth century, Richard Wright, in a relatively brief lifetime (1908–1960), made the transition from the grandson of slave grandparents in rural Mississippi to an up-and-coming author in Chicago, to the celebrated author of *Native Son* (1940) in New York City, to a writer of international status in Paris in the late 1940s and on into the 1950s. While he never stopped learning and growing, he remained faithful to his vision of personal freedom as the ideal for everyone. His own experience growing up in various parts of the South taught him that society was based on the control of its individual members, whether that control used race, religion, social class, politics, the family, or anything else. Wright was unsuited to control of any type, because his desire for autonomy was extremely strong.

Born into circumstances that may not have been as unpropitious as he claims in his autobiography, *Black Boy* (this necessarily brief biographical sketch is based on *Black Boy* and Michel Fabre's *The Unfinished Quest of Richard Wright*, 1993), published in an expurgated version in 1945 and in an uncensored edition in 1991, Wright nevertheless was faced with daunting barriers to literary achievement: racism, poverty, family problems, religion, and a modest formal education. To be born black in Mississippi in 1908, when accurate records of the time of birth of black children were not kept in that state, was to be denied most opportunities for literary accomplishment, although Wright is obviously an exception. In 1908, black Mississippians could not vote, live where they wanted to, attend white schools (which were much better financed than black ones), or ride on integrated train cars. Wright's parents, Nathan (an illiterate farmer) and Ella Wright (a schoolteacher whose parents thought she had married "down"), never had enough money to properly feed and clothe their two sons, Richard and his younger brother Leon Alan, and Nathan made matters much worse by abandoning his wife and children for another woman when Richard was just a little boy. Wright's father is viewed negatively throughout Chapter 1 of *Black Boy*. His son sees him as a glutton when he eats (readers have noted the completely negative description of Mr. Wright eating in the first chapter) and as a tyrant who ordered his two sons to keep quiet during the daytime so he could sleep (he worked as a night porter). The younger Wright took his father's command to keep a meowing kitten quiet by literally killing it in order to make his father feel resentment toward him.

As a young boy, Wright learned the power of words to inflict damage on his enemies. When Wright jumps 25 years ahead of his narrative at the end of the first chapter of *Black Boy*, he looks down on his father as a "black peasant," who is illiterate, poor, and toothless. Part of his dislike of his father seems to be class based, although few sons are going to forgive fathers who walk out on family responsibilities. Pointing out to Wright that his father's behavior could be explained but not justified (how many people would want to be a night porter, one of the few jobs open to black men in the early twentieth century?) would hardly have made him feel any warmer toward Mr. Wright. Part of the problem between them also was the fact that both the older and the younger Wright wanted their own way. It can be suggestive to compare Wright's depiction of families in his fiction to his presentation of his own family. He may at times be compensating.

However, Wright's childhood was not completely negative. There were books in his house, and his mother had been a schoolteacher. She also encouraged him and taught him how to read. One morning, the coal man taught him to count to 100. As a boy, Wright also roamed around the various neighborhoods in which he lived, trying to satisfy his relentless curiosity about the world, a curiosity that persisted until his death. One particularly amusing instance of it was his watching, with a crowd of other black children, the "opened rear ends" (21) of outdoor privies used by numerous black and white adults. Wright and his young friends would spend hours observing and commenting on various physiological and excremental details of what they saw. Eventually, a white policeman was posted to put an end to the children's amusement. Perhaps the strongest counterevidence to Wright's negative view of the black community is that if it was so bleak, how did it manage to produce *Black Boy* and his many other literary accomplishments?

Positive boyhood experiences would further include his intense appreciation for nature. Early in Chapter 1 of *Black Boy*, he cites horses, dew, the Mississippi River, wild geese, burning hickory wood, prideful sparrows, a solitary ant, and much more as indications of nature's appeal to the lyrical side of his sensibility. It is also clear that he learned a great deal about folk culture while he was growing up. For instance, he learned that if he put a hair from a horse's tail into a jar of urine, it would be transformed into a snake. Or that he could turn himself into a girl by kissing his elbow. Or that lightning would not hit him if he covered a mirror during a storm. When he was able to attend school, he was very much one of the boys, as when he refused to tell on who it was that was shelling walnuts in his Aunt Addie's schoolroom, because that would have violated the male code. He had friends who helped him get jobs and taught him the ways of white folks. One of them, a young man named Griggs, once yanked him out of the way of some passing whites so Wright would understand what they expected of him. They expected him to anticipate their slightest whims in a manner that indicated his total acknowledgement of their "superiority."

On the negative side of things, probably what was most traumatic to the young Wright was what happened to him when he accidentally set his grandparents' house on fire: his recollection is that the person to whom he most often turned for affection, his mother, beat him nearly to death. She was unable to give him the amount of love he craved because of several paralytic strokes. The resulting suffering came to represent the futility of so much human unhappiness in Wright's mind.

Although the young Richard Wright lived in a nearly all-black world, he did experience white racism during his youth. One day, a car occupied by young white men offered to let him hold on while he was riding his bicycle. The car pulled him along until one of the whites smashed a bottle in his face, which caused him to crash his bike. He then had to endure their racial taunts out of fear that they might do something worse to him if he did not. On another occasion, he was being considered for work at a white woman's house, when she asked him if he stole or not. Assuming this conversation actually happened, we are provided with an instance of a white person believing Wright was so stupid that he might actually admit to stealing. Although the young Wright never witnessed racially motivated white violence, he did learn of the killing of his Uncle Hoskins by whites who coveted his lucrative saloon business, and he knew all too well that white privileges in the South were backed by the constant threat of lynching.

Because of the lack of money in his family, Wright sometimes went without food (hunger of various sorts is a persistent theme in his work) and could not afford clothes for school. One of the reasons he disliked his father is that he blamed him for his mother's financial plight. Another source of stress in the young Wright's life was his maternal grandmother and her Seventh-Day Adventism, something to which she insisted he conform. Doing so, however, meant he could not work on Saturdays, the day of worship for Seventh-Day Adventists, or read worldly books—indeed, his grandmother once threw a boarder out of her house for reading *Bluebeard and His Seven Wives* to her grandson. Wright was deeply affected by her excluding him from the imaginary world of Bluebeard. Even though he rejected her religion, it reappears in secularized form throughout his literary career. The recipient of a ninth-grade formal education, he was largely self-educated, becoming an incessant reader and traveler for the rest of his life. When still a teenager, he wrote a tale titled "The Voodoo of Hell's Half-Acre," published with the shortened title "Hell's Half-Acre" in the Jackson, Mississippi, *Southern Register.* Also as a teenager, he read the iconoclast H. L. Mencken, who amazed him with his forceful attacks on the South; it was then that Wright realized words could be weapons, a keynote of his own writing style and career.

Through a series of odd jobs and petty crimes, he was able to leave the South, in a geographical sense, for Chicago, where he arrived in 1927, at the age of 19. He spent the next decade of his life there, helping the Communist Party, scratching out a living, making the transition to an urbanized lifestyle, but most of all, learning how to write. His early efforts include poems such as "I Have Seen Black Hands" that were inspired by his Marxist sympathies, retained even after he left the

Communist Party because it tried to tell him how to write. His persistence in reading his new environment in terms of his old one resulted in his needlessly lying to the Hoffmans, a couple who employed him as a delivery boy for their delicatessen. The year the Great Depression began, 1929, he got a job at the Chicago post office after a desperate attempt to increase his weight to the necessary minimum. In Chicago, he also started writing a novel titled *Cesspool,* which was published posthumously in 1963 under the title *Lawd Today!* In 1931, he published a short story, "Superstition," in *Abbott's Monthly Magazine.* As much as he hated to do it, Wright was eventually forced to accept public assistance in order to survive. Later, he worked in the Michael Reese Hospital, cleaning up after mice and rabbits, which, because of a fight between two of his coworkers, got put back in the wrong cages. Wright often wondered later what effects this had on the medical experiments that involved these animals.

While he was in Chicago, he also joined the John Reed Club, which was a key development in his determination to become a writer. With support from the Communist Party, this club enabled Wright to publish revolutionary poetry for a sympathetic, largely white audience. He rapidly became a rising star in the progressive literary circle in Chicago, regularly publishing poetry in Communist journals. In 1934, he accepted a job as supervisor in a club for young black men, an experience that would help him write *Native Son.* At this time, he also read such important American authors as Theodore Dreiser, Sherwood Anderson, and Gertrude Stein, the latter of whom would later befriend him in Paris. The next year, he started writing a story that many readers regard as one of his most successful, "Big Boy Leaves Home," and he also wrote what many of his admirers regard as his best poem, a horrifying recreation of a lynching titled "Between the World and Me."

He started doing journalistic work at about this time, covering the victory of the great black heavyweight Joe Louis over the German champion, Max Baer, for *New Masses.* The journalistic strain would be heard again in the 1950s, most notably, when he visited Spain and Indonesia, out of which emerged *Pagan Spain* and *The Color Curtain.* During the mid-1930s, he also took part in the Negro Federal Theater of Chicago, marking the beginning of a sustained interest in the stage. Two of his novels, *Native Son* and *The Long Dream,* in fact, would eventually be turned into plays for commercial production. During this period as well, he joined the South Side Writers' Group, which included Arna Bontemps, the author of *Black Thunder*, and Margaret Walker, who would later write a controversial biography of Wright that appeared in 1988.

In 1937, he ended his relationship with the Communist Party in Chicago, because it wanted him to keep tabs on the price of food, whereas he wanted to write as he saw fit. Refusing to be treated as he had been in the South, he decided to move to New York City this same year in an effort to satisfy his literary ambitions. Before he was 30, then, he had spent almost 20 years in various parts of the South, as well as a decade in the urban North. His experiences in both times and places would serve him well, especially when he came to write his two best-known books, *Native Son* and *Black Boy*.

In New York City, he published an important essay, "Blueprint for Negro Writing," which, while critical of African American writing, reveals that he did not know a great deal about it. There, he also met Ralph Ellison, whom he encouraged and who would later write *Invisible Man*, and Paul Reynolds Jr., who would become his literary agent and a close friend and supporter. Because of Reynolds's efforts, Wright's first published book, *Uncle Tom's Children* (1938), was placed with Harper and Brothers, thus marking the beginning of a long relationship between Wright and Harper. *Uncle Tom's Children*, though, disappointed its young author, in that the reaction among many readers was sentimental. He corrected this response by writing *Native Son*, a novel dominated by a young black man. Wright wanted to cause fear rather than tears in his readers. The response to *Uncle Tom's Children* by black reviewers was positive, with the notable exception of Zora Neale Hurston, the author of *Their Eyes Were Watching God*, which Wright had severely criticized when he reviewed it. The two disagreed about each other's work because she celebrated black folk values, whereas Wright gave much more attention than she did to white racism and the violence it could cause. Other black critics, such as Alain Locke and Sterling Brown, were more positive in their reactions to *Uncle Tom's Children*. White reviewers were generally upbeat, especially if they shared Wright's sympathy for Marxism.

His personal life also took some dramatic turns in New York. Michel Fabre, his primary biographer, describes his near marriage to his landlady's daughter, broken off because, he asserted, she had congenital syphilis. He also became involved with two other women, Dhima Rose Meadman, a dance teacher, and Ellen Poplar, the latter of whom he loved. He apparently misinterpreted her caution in deciding whether or not to marry a black man as a rebuff and instead married Dhima; Ralph Ellison was his best man. This first marriage ended quickly, in 1940. The next year, he married Ellen, who was an active member of the Communist Party. They had two daughters, Julia and Rachel, the former of whom has written *Daughter of a Native Son*, expected to appear in 2000.

When Harper and Brothers published *Native Son* in 1940, Wright rapidly became the most famous black writer in the United States. A best-seller, it was a warning as well about what could happen if the country continued to refuse to face the truth about how African Americans feel about the way whites treat them. Made into two films, the first starring Wright himself as the central character, Bigger Thomas, the book is frequently taught and cited as one of the most important books published in the United States in the twentieth century. In Bigger Thomas, Wright created a nightmarish warning of what is being produced in the urban ghettoes. He never again wrote such a powerful book. *Native Son* was very well received by the general reader (it was a Book-of-the-Month Club selection) and by most professional reviewers. Such mainstream white critics as Malcolm Cowley were very enthusiastic, while black readers praised it but were also leery that such an aggressive protagonist as Bigger Thomas would confirm white stereotypes about black men. In a matter of weeks, *Native Son* was topping the charts: it was truly an overnight sensation.

On his way back to Chicago after a trip to Mexico with his first wife, Wright, traveling alone, stopped off in Mississippi to visit his father, whom he had not seen in a quarter of a century. In *Black Boy*, he is at pains to let readers know he did not end up like his father—a poor, ignorant sharecropper. During this time, he also collaborated with the playwright Paul Green on an adaptation of *Native Son* for the stage. Furthermore, he started to work on *Twelve Million Black Voices* (1941), a folk history of black people. Although only several thousand copies of this history were originally printed, it was very well received. Arna Bontemps, the distinguished author, particularly admired it. Also in the early 1940s, he published one of his most frequently anthologized short stories, "Almos' a Man," later made into a short film with LeVar Burton portraying the protagonist, Dave Saunders. In 1942, Wright wrote "The Man Who Lived Underground," one of his most satisfying and provocative works of fiction, as well as a transition from the mostly naturalist mode of *Native Son* to modernism. Although the United States had entered World War II by then, he was not drafted because he was the only source of financial support for his family.

In 1943, Wright penned what may be his most satisfying book, *Black Boy*, published in a censored version in 1945 and in an unexpurgated edition version in 1991. (Although some readers have assumed the 1991 version is superior because it is uncensored, that may not necessarily be the case.) Regarding both editions, attempts have been made to keep the book from being taught. Both versions are fictionalized; that is, they are artistic interpretations of Wright's early life rather than strictly factual records of it. He depicts himself as a strong-willed, very bright, imaginative, and hypersensitive African American who triumphed over an ugly world. Like *Native Son*, it became a best-seller and was also a Book-of-the-Month Club selection. It was acclaimed by both professional white literary critics and by many black and white readers, although the great black writer and thinker W.E.B. Du Bois was offended by some of the language. Communist reviewers were negative because by the time *Black Boy* appeared in 1945, Wright had broken with the Communist Party. Some other black general readers and reviewers did not want to hear the truth about the situation into which Southern blacks had been forced. The issue of whether or not he had now done his best work is still not resolved. Part of the problem is that his books after 1945 (he did not publish another one until 1953, when *The Outsider* appeared) are written in modes different from the ones in which his two best-known books are composed. It may not be reasonable to compare the many books he published in the last seven years of his life to his earlier work, because he was not trying to write in that tradition —namely, the racial protest tradition—again, although *The Long Dream* (1958) may be an exception. The issue of whether or not Wright hurt himself as a writer by moving to Paris is also still unresolved.

In terms of his personal friendships at this point in his career, the same year *Black Boy* appeared, 1945, Wright helped a young James Baldwin win a fellowship. Unfortunately, their friendship ended in acrimony, with Baldwin attacking Wright in several essays. It is possible that Baldwin felt the need to kick against Wright as a father figure, the way sons sometimes establish their autonomy from their fathers. Ralph Ellison, too, denied what appears to be literary indebtedness when one puts his *Invisible Man* next to Wright's "The Man Who Lived Underground."

Wright also befriended Chester Himes, who wrote *If He Hollers Let Him Go* and who remained a lifelong friend to Wright.

After World War II ended, the French government invited Wright to visit Paris. His acceptance led to another turning point in his life: moving to Europe with his family. Much debate has centered on the issue of whether or not Wright's "exile," if that is the appropriate term, resulted in inferior work. In France, he was celebrated as a great author, hailed by such important writers and thinkers as Jean-Paul Sartre (the existentialist philosopher), Simone de Beauvoir (the French feminist), and the aforementioned Gertrude Stein (a U.S. expatriate whose work Wright held in high regard). He also became active in the *Négritude* circle, a movement that concentrated on celebrating blackness and freeing black Africa from European political and cultural imperialism.

By 1947, Wright decided to move to Paris with his family for an extended period. He did not want Julia to be subjected to the racial humiliation he knew she would experience in the United States. By this point in his life, he had become a writer of international status, with his work being translated into many European languages and with great social demands made on his time and energy. He had come a long way from his earliest days in Mississippi. Very few other people could have made such an intellectual and geographical journey, and yet, as Baldwin once said, Wright remained a black Mississippian wherever he was. He eventually came to see the plight of black people in the United States as a microcosmic version of the global problems people of color face.

The year 1949 is notable in Wright's life for several reasons: it was the year in which his other daughter, Rachel, was born, and it was then that he wrote the film script for *Native Son*. Turning this powerful novel into a movie was an important project to him. Unfortunately, the first film version of *Native Son* (the one starring Wright himself as Bigger Thomas) is not very successful as a film. Ironically, the once undernourished Wright now had to lose weight to look like the 20-year-old Bigger. Wright is more curious than compelling in the role. Nevertheless, the making of the movie took up much of his time, energy, and money. It was filmed mostly in Argentina under the direction of Pierre Chenal, and substantial cuts were made from it before it appeared in theaters in the United States in 1951.

As preoccupied as Wright was with this cinematic project, he did not cease writing at midcentury; indeed, he worked sporadically on *The*

Outsider until 1952. When it was finally published the next year, it generated far less impact than had *Native Son*. In fact, the reception was largely negative. Professional reviewers objected to the long philosophical speeches, the coincidences in the plot, the wooden characters. Sales were far below those of *Native Son* and *Black Boy*. Yet Wright endured, spending most of the summer in what is now known as Ghana (formerly Africa's Gold Coast). The result is a book called *Black Power*, which argues that Ghana would have to industrialize to catch up with the West. Wright views the Africans through Western eyes in this work, never really accepting animism and other African traditions. As an agnostic, Western, secular rationalist, Wright was not really predisposed to understand the people he met in Ghana. Not many copies of *Black Power* were printed, but most reviews were positive, although there were fewer than there had been for *Black Boy* and *Native Son*. The market for such a book among general readers was small.

Wright again traveled in the summer of 1954, this time visiting Spain, a trip that resulted in another travel book, *Pagan Spain*, published in 1957. Although few general readers bought it, the reviews were fairly positive. The reviewer for the *Christian Science Monitor* noted that "a great deal of what the author says both is true and urgently needs saying" (February 21, 1957, 13). Writing in the *Jackson Daily News*, another writer said it was "vigorous, compassionate and engrossing" (February 24, 1957). Wright also published a novel in 1954, *Savage Holiday*, based on the life of a man who accidentally locks himself out of his apartment and ends up killing the mother of a boy whose death he unintentionally causes. It was published as a paperback original and received no reviews. During this same period, Wright became close friends with his Dutch translator, Margrit de Sablonière.

The middle of the decade found Wright continuing his global traveling by attending the Bandung Conference in Indonesia, a meeting of so-called Third World nations determined to resist Western dominance. This trip resulted in *The Color Curtain: A Report on the Bandung Conference* (1956). Reviews were generally good, but they were mostly by people who attended the conference or by specialists in Asian affairs. The reviewer for *The Progressive* felt Wright lacked adequate background knowledge. The next year saw the publication of a collection of essays, *White Man, Listen!*, which was not reviewed very widely or favorably in the white press but which black reviewers were quite positive toward.

Roi Ottley, for example, said in "few works has he [Wright] risen to such reasoned passion," in the *Chicago Sunday Tribune Magazine of Books* (November 10, 1957, 11). Overall, though, none of Wright's works of nonfiction were very popular with general readers.

In terms of his fiction, throughout this period, he had been working on a novel set in Mississippi, *The Long Dream* (1958), which revolves around the relationship between Tyree, a black businessman, and his son Fishbelly. Several reviewers argued that Wright had lost touch with his Southern roots and needed to return home, at least for a visit. More specifically, the writer for *Commonweal* stated that *The Long Dream* "would seem to provide little insight on current U.S. interracial realities" (69 [October 31, 1958], 131). He next produced a sequel to *The Long Dream* titled *Island of Hallucinations*, which is unfinished and unpublished, although excerpts have appeared. In them, Fishbelly's experiences in the black community in Paris are related. They seem to reflect Wright's own suspicions and doubts about some of his black acquaintances in Paris, who Wright feared were working for the U.S. government at a time when it suspected that Communist agents were hiding under every bed. Wright became so disillusioned with the atmosphere in France that he decided to settle in England, where Ellen and his two daughters were. His troubles in trying to obtain a visa precluded his carrying out this plan, but he did find consolation in trying his hand at haiku, a delicate Japanese verse form of 17 syllables. Many of these have been collected and recently published.

The last year of Wright's remarkable life is noteworthy for several reasons, one of which was his depression over money at the time. His writings no longer generated the income they once did, and he was supporting two households, one in Paris, the other in England. He also finished proofreading a collection of short stories, *Eight Men*, that was published posthumously. Reviewers were ignorant of the fact that two of the stories, "Man of All Work" and "Man, God Ain't Like That," were radio plays, so there was some confusion about them. But the writer for the *New York Times Book Review* found all eight stories "beautifully, pitifully, terribly true" (January 22, 1961, 5). The reviewer for the *New Republic* singled out "The Man Who Lived Underground" as "satisfying both for its tense surface and its elasticity of suggestion" (144 [February 13, 1961], 17). Two important black readers, Nick Aaron Ford and

Saunders Redding, were unenthusiastic. Few general readers bought *Eight Men.*

Two other books appeared posthumously as well: *Lawd Today!* and *American Hunger.* The former did not receive much attention when it was published in 1963, but the review in *Library Journal* on April 1 of that year did say it was an "important book," although Nick Aaron Ford doubted Wright had written it. By 1977, when *American Hunger* appeared, interest in Wright had revived, and so it attracted considerable attention, even though most of it had already been published in excerpts. The reviewer for the *Nashville Banner* claimed it stood out "like a priceless gem" (May 14, 1977). And the reviewer for the *Chicago Sun-Times Book Week* described *American Hunger* as "a moving memoir of the process which led to the emergence of a major writer" (May 29, 1977, 7).

Many people were surprised when Wright died of a heart attack after a routine medical test in a Parisian hospital in the fall of 1960. There has been speculation that he was actually assassinated by the Central Intelligence Agency, but Wright's foremost biographer has found no evidence to support this view. When he died in his early fifties, his popularity in the United States had fallen. Now, however, his work is widely considered essential reading for anyone who wants to understand some of the key changes in the societal history of the United States, especially in regard to African American experience in the twentieth century. While certainly not the only view of this experience, Wright's is one of the most powerful, as well as one of the most brightly revealing.

Richard Wright's Literary Heritage

Wright explored the possibilities of a variety of thematic and stylistic traditions, but he is most acclaimed for work that examines one theme in the category of fiction (his autobiography is subtitled "A Record of Childhood and Youth," but it, like most other autobiographies, is fictionalized to some extent and can be treated along with his other works of fiction). Specifically, in almost every work of prose fiction he wrote, a male protagonist is confronted by a hostile environment. This theme is one of the oldest in Western literature, going back at least as far as Homer in ancient Greece. But Wright gives it a powerful racial spin, revealing how skin color complicates the already challenging trial of manhood. He excavated this rich vein of literary ore by means of the three traditions of realism, naturalism, and modernism. Such broad terms can be more precisely calibrated as to how they bear particularly on Wright's fiction: it is realistic in the sense that it rejects what he perceived to be the softer, romantic treatment of African American experience by the writers of the Harlem Renaissance during the 1920s. It is naturalistic in that it depicts, particularly in *Native Son*, life for black Americans as set in a jungle, a site of murderous competition for survival. On the other hand, Wright was influenced by literary modernism as well as realism and naturalism. Modernism emphasizes myth, symbolism, and the irrational, as can be readily observed in two of its most famous representative samples, T. S. Eliot's *The Waste Land* and James Joyce's *Ulysses*. Wright's apprentice novel, *Lawd Today!*, alludes to the former and restricts its action to one day in the life of the central character, as does Joyce's novel. Wright was also impressed by another icon of literary modernism, Gertrude Stein, whose character of Melanctha in *Three Lives* he particularly admired as one of the few convincing portraits of a black woman by a white writer. He was also intrigued by Stein's experiments with individual sentences. It may be that the reason Bigger Thomas is perplexed by Mr. Dalton's paintings is that they are modernist, and the use of symbolic overtones in naturalism, as in the case of *Native Son*, hints at another way in which Wright borrowed from modernism. Like most writers, Wright visited generic and thematic endowments for what he needed for his own literary purposes.

His first published book, *Uncle Tom's Children* (1938), revises Harriet Beecher Stowe's *Uncle Tom's Cabin* (1852), in which the black male protagonist is passive and sexless. Stowe wanted slavery abolished; she knew that an assertive, sexually active black man in the role of Uncle Tom could have alienated white readers and reinforced a threatening stereotype. Wright revises her novel in his collection to display an assertive black manhood. But since some white readers responded with tears to *Uncle Tom's Children*, he revised it, too, in *Native Son* to include a killer named Bigger Thomas, over whom no reader would cry. Bigger smothers a white woman to whom he is sexually attracted and smashes in the head of a black woman upon whom he has forced himself.

Uncle Tom's Children begins with a short story, "Big Boy Leaves Home," that might be considered quintessential Wright: it treats the experiences of a black male protagonist in a realistic-naturalistic mode with modernist overtones. What would have been a lighthearted excursion by four adolescents playing hooky in a sentimental literary tradition Wright shapes into a deadly tale of sexual paranoia with mythical resonance. In the story, Big Boy Morrison and his three friends intend merely to go swimming in a white man's swimming hole, but because a white woman sees them naked, several people are killed, including one of Big Boy's friends. Racial violence was one of Wright's recurring themes: from the beginning of his career to the end, he posed the question of why someone should be killed because he or she is black.

This same collection includes three stories—"Down by the River-side," "Fire and Cloud," and "Bright and Morning Star"—that are written in the realist vein and celebrate black folks, although the heroes in the first two are individual black males, and an individual black woman is the heroine in the third. The turn to celebrations and explorations of the black folk community in fiction can be seen in the work of other African American novelists at the same time *Uncle Tom's Children* appeared: Arna Bontemps's *Black Thunder* (1936), William Attaway's *Blood on the Forge* (1941), and Zora Neale Hurston's *Their Eyes Were Watching God* (1937). Rather than concentrating on the so-called talented tenth of black people that W.E.B. Du Bois focuses on in the earlier *The Souls of Black Folk* (1903), these books, along with Wright's, emphasize the power of the black community as a whole. Although Wright did not approve of Hurston's novel, he did admire *Black Thunder* and *Blood on the Forge*. Bontemps re-created a slave revolt led by Gabriel Prosser in Virginia in 1800. Many of the whites cannot understand that Gabriel and his followers are only doing what the whites would have done had they been enslaved. This is the same point missed by so many of the whites in *Native Son*. Bigger Thomas does what many of them would have done if they had been in his position. Like Gabriel Prosser, too, Bigger ends up executed. Wright was sympathetic to Attaway's novel because of its powerful depiction of black folks whose lives have been deformed by industrialization. The one other tale in the *Uncle Tom's Children*, "Long Black Song," examines the crisis a black woman faces after being victimized by a white sexual predator.

Native Son (1940) emerges from the rich tradition of African American folk experience and from the kind of naturalism Wright found in Theodore Dreiser's *An American Tragedy* (1925). Dreiser places his protagonist, Clyde Griffiths, in a highly detailed social context to explain his behavior, especially regarding the drowning of a young woman. Wright uses a similar strategy to account for the murderous hatred of whites on the part of his black protagonist in *Native Son*. The bold innovation on Wright's part is the *apparent* confirmation of white stereotypes about black males: you whites are correct, Wright suggests, in taking Bigger to be the embodiment of black rage, but whom do you blame for that? Like Clyde, Bigger is a product of a social environment he did not create. In *Native Son*, Wright bends the naturalistic novel into a shape that directs readers to look for responsibility for black anger in the white community. He also borrows effectively from the traditions of detective fiction, Gothic romance, and protest literature.

Certainly, *Native Son* can be read as a detective novel, with the hard-bitten Britten, who works for Bigger's employer, Mr. Dalton, clearly indebted to a tradition in which detectives are not much different from criminals. The exciting chase scenes in Book Two of *Native Son* reveal Wright's relish in exploiting another element of detective fiction, as thousands of police officers chase Bigger in Chicago's Black Belt. As for Gothic romance, Kate, the Daltons' white cat, and the furnace in the Daltons' basement indicate Wright's fondness for the tradition Edgar Allan Poe and Nathaniel Hawthorne explored so successfully. Poe even wrote a short story about a black cat, the color of which Wright has changed for his own purposes in *Native Son*. Wright's innovation in the tradition of Gothic romance is to give horror and mystery, the staples of the tradition, a racial twist. Kate is photographed sitting on Bigger's shoulder, which suggests his anxiety and guilt about the smothering, decapitating, and incinerating of Mary Dalton. The eerie atmosphere of the Daltons' basement, with its glowing furnace, recalls the darkness and mystery in Hawthorne and Poe. Finally, Wright's debt to the protest tradition in U.S. literature can be seen clearly in *Black Boy* in his recognition of H. L. Mencken's use of language to protest authority and prejudice, particularly in the latter's *A Book of Prefaces*. In many ways, such protest is what Wright's fiction is all about, but with a much more salient racial emphasis than can be found in Mencken.

As to why Wright himself did not turn out to be Bigger Thomas, *Black Boy* (1945, 1991) provides the answer. It is one of the most highly regarded U.S. autobiographies and draws on the country's autobiographical tradition in which a (usually male) protagonist overcomes daunting obstacles to achieve success. Wright casts himself in the role of a hero beleaguered on all sides who still manages to prevail. Like such forebears as Benjamin Franklin, Frederick Douglass, Booker T. Washington, and W.E.B. Du Bois, Wright relies mainly on his own resources. The powerfully seductive theme of individualism informs every page of *Black Boy*, as it does so much of the literature of the United States. If anyone's selfhood is strong enough, one can overcome anything: willpower is everything. Wright turned frustrations that drove Bigger to commit two murders into autobiographical art. Wright follows the formula for successful self-realization as a male to the letter. He relies on himself rather than other people or social institutions. He, like his models, is a self-made man. Writing to this blueprint was his salvation.

Eight years passed before Wright published another book. *The Outsider* (1953) is written in an existentialist mode, although Wright had developed an existentialist sensibility long before he wrote this work. Existentialism can be defined in numerous ways, but an inclusive definition might be encapsulated in the statement that values are not given but created. We determine what matters; it is not dictated to us by some ultimate authority. Wright's protagonist in *The Outsider*, Cross Damon, misinterprets this notion into thinking that anything is allowed. Wright counters this conclusion with overwhelming evidence that some social constraints are unavoidable; otherwise, the Cross Damons of this social world would destroy the social world. Cross Damon occupies a place in a venerable tradition in Western literature: that of the figure willing to challenge the limits upon which societies insist. An example from the Renaissance literary period would be the English playwright Christopher Marlowe's Dr. Faustus, who agrees to exchange his soul in return for godlike knowledge. More recent examples would be the nineteenth-century English poet Samuel Taylor Coleridge's Ancient Mariner in *The Rime of the Ancient Mariner*, who, because he committed the unspeakable crime of killing an albatross, must wander the earth, telling those he meets what he has done. Later in the nineteenth century, the Russian novelist Fyodor Dostoyevsky, in a novel titled *Crime and Punishment*, examined the consequences of an arbitrary murder committed by its protagonist. Just a few years before *The Outsider* appeared, the French existentialist Albert Camus published *The Stranger*, which examines an apparently gratuitous murder. Wright's contribution to this tradition, Cross Damon, makes an overwhelming case for the necessity of social conventions.

The next year, Wright published his only paperback original, a short novel called *Savage Holiday* (1954), which has white characters instead of black ones. It reveals his profound debt to Freudianism, as Erskine Caldwell, the central character, commits a brutal murder caused by his subconscious anxiety about his mother. As a psychoanalytic novel, *Savage Holiday* is part of the modernist literary tradition, which emphasizes the irrational and the subconscious. The same year *Savage Holiday* appeared, Wright began publishing in rapid succession a series of travel books—*Black Power*, *The Color Curtain*, and *Pagan Spain*—as well as a collection of essays, *White Man, Listen!* Then he turned to black experience in the South again, with *The Long Dream* (1958), which was to have been the first volume in a trilogy, but the project was never finished. This novel focuses on a father-son relationship in the South and was written in the naturalist mode with modernist overtones.

Part of the next novel in the trilogy, *Island of Hallucinations*, was published in 1963 after Wright died, under the title "Five Episodes." Set in Paris, these excerpts seem to reflect some of Wright's experiences among black expatriates in France in the 1950s. The first one features a humorous misunderstanding about a colorful hat the character Fish wears in Paris; he thinks the crowd that is so intrigued by his hat is after *him*, the way a lynch mob would have been in the United States. The next episode turns on a funny incident in which Fish thinks a French woman is preventing him from getting her table at a restaurant out of racism, when she is actually looking for false teeth under the table. The third episode deals with the concept of Afrocentricity, and the penultimate one with a black woman in Paris who flatters rich white Americans into giving her money. The final episode relates the sexual adventures of a black man who exploits white women. The published excerpts from *Island of Hallucinations* show Wright investigating new literary territory for him: black men from the South in France.

Since Wright's death in 1960, four more of his books have appeared: *Eight Men* (1961), *Lawd Today!* (1963), *American Hunger* (1977), and *Rite of Passage* (1994). The first volume—a collection of five short stories, two radio plays, and an autobiographical sketch—demonstrates the variety of Wright's styles and themes from early in his career until the end. It is written in his realist-naturalist mode ("The Man Who Saw the Flood"), as well as in a modernist style ("The Man Who Lived Underground"). It touches on many of his most familiar thematic bases, too, from Freudianism ("The Man Who Killed a Shadow"), to autobiography ("The Man Who Went to Chicago"), to colonialism ("Man, God Ain't Like That"). *Lawd Today!* is an apprentice novel written much earlier than its date of publication. It deals with the theme of the utter futility of the life of the central character and owes a big debt to James Joyce's *Ulysses*, a modernist icon. *Eight Men* is, in what it says and in how it says it, quintessential Wright. *American Hunger* is the part of *Black Boy* that was omitted from the original edition, published in 1945. Most of it had been published in various parts before 1977, but *American Hunger* did collect them together for the first time. In 1991, *Black Boy* was published with both parts, one set in the South and the other in Chicago, combined for the first time. The most recently published volume, *Rite of Passage*, originally titled *The Jackal*, was written in 1945 but not published until 1994. Set in Harlem, it narrates the experiences of 15-year-old Johnny Gibbs, who is taken from his foster family for bureaucratic reasons and, as a result, joins a gang called The Moochers. Unlike Bigger Thomas, Johnny is well adjusted to his community and a good student, with a happy home life, until he is ejected from his family. When this happens, he finds another family by prevailing in a ferocious fight with Baldy, the leader of The Moochers. The gang then robs a white man, and as the boys run away, Johnny thinks he hears the voice of a black woman calling out after him. Whether or not he actually hears the voice, Wright is calling out to the boys and to the world to pay attention to what is happening to young black men in the United States.

Rather than adding innovations to his stylistic heritage, Wright chose to bend it to suit his thematic needs. Realism, naturalism, modernism, the Gothic romance, detective fiction, and the protest tradition all provided him with a literary endowment from which he could borrow to dramatize, in disturbing and unforgettable ways, the plight of black women and men in the United States and throughout the world. For three decades, Wright analyzed the effects of denying freedom to African Americans and oppressed people of color everywhere, the most remarkable of these being Bigger Thomas and Richard Wright himself.

3

Uncle Tom's Children
(1938, 1940)

Uncle Tom's Children, Wright's revision of Harriet Beecher Stowe's famous novel, *Uncle Tom's Cabin* (1852), appeared first in 1938, and again in 1940, the latter edition adding a fifth short story, "Bright and Morning Star." As a counter to Stowe's asexual, saintly Uncle Tom, Wright offers us a number of mostly credible and assertive black men, and some black women, who resist oppression rather than engage in passive suffering. The sentimental reaction to *Uncle Tom's Children* by some readers at the time of its first publication led to Wright's determination to create in his next published book, *Native Son*, a novel about which no one would feel sentimental. *Uncle Tom's Children* opens with the autobiographical sketch "The Ethics of Living Jim Crow," which will not be examined here because most of it reappears in expanded form in *Black Boy.* After the sketch, Wright quotes a once popular song beginning with the line "Is it true what they say about Dixie?," which muses about the many potential sources of happiness in the South. If what people say about the South is true, then the narrator says that is where she or he belongs. For *Uncle Tom's Children* denies that the claim contains any truth for blacks.

"BIG BOY LEAVES HOME"

PLOT DEVELOPMENT

The first short story in the collection, and one that many readers regard as one of Wright's best short stories, "Big Boy Leaves Home," is based on a powerful disjunction between what should have been a day of fun for four young black men and what happens instead. The title prepares us for the contradiction in that it suggests a young man leaving the nest, but Big Boy's "leaving" is actually a terrified escape from a lynching. Comprised of five parts and set in the South, the tale begins with four young black men—Big Boy Morrison, Buck, Bobo, and Lester—engaging in nothing more sinister than playing hooky from school. Wright emphasizes the Edenic nature of their outlook when he describes how they catch and pull "long green blades of grass with their toes" (420). They play "the dozens" (an African American verbal contest in which the goal is to insult the opponent's mother without losing control when one's own mother is insulted). But underneath the initial fun lay persistent references to trains heading north, the same direction Big Boy will be headed the next morning on his brother's truck as he flees in terror from a place that is anything but a paradise.

On their way to a swimming hole, Big Boy's three companions wrestle him to the ground in jest, but he starts choking Bobo and demands that Bobo tell Lester and Buck to get off him, a strategy that succeeds. Claiming to be a "smart nigger," Big Boy thrusts out his chest as he takes pleasure in his belief that when you are attacked by many, you should attack one of the many with everything you have, which will result in the many backing off. Big Boy will soon learn how ineffective such a tactic is when he and Bobo are chased by a lynch mob later the same day.

In Part II, they arrive at the swimming hole. Bobo does not want to go swimming because old man Harvey, the owner, will not allow black people in it, and Lester relates that Harvey took a shot at Bobo (apparently a friend of theirs) for swimming in it. Lester also reads aloud the No Trespassing sign to the others. Nevertheless, all the boys undress to prepare for their swim. But a sunny idyll is about to end: the snake in this garden is not diabolical but a white woman named Bertha, Harvey's daughter-in-law; Bertha means "bright" in German, a quiet irony in a story about four dark-skinned young men. In contrast to the stereotype of the black man as rapist of white women, Big Boy and his three pals "instinctively" cover "their groins" (249) when they see Bertha. Terrified, the four swimmers are not sure what they should do, but just as Big Boy and Lester decide to get their clothes, Bertha screams for Jim, her husband and old man Harvey's son. Stopping three feet from her (she, interestingly, is standing near their clothes), Big Boy tells her that they want their clothes back. Bobo grabs them, but Jim shoots Lester and then Buck, killing them both. When Jim next tries to shoot Bobo, Big Boy seizes the barrel of his gun and Jim flings him to the ground in response, at which point Bobo jumps onto Jim's back. After hitting Jim in the mouth with the rifle barrel, Big Boy shoots and kills him. As Big Boy and Bobo flee through the woods, a previously friendly nature turns hostile: "Vines and leaves switched their faces" (252).

In Part III, Big Boy arrives at the home he knows he must now leave, a home that will soon be set on fire by angry whites. His father gets word to some of the leaders of his family's church to come to the Morrisons' house to help formulate a plan to save Big Boy's life. They decide he should flee to Chicago the next morning in a truck driven by his brother Will, who works for the ironically named Magnolia Express Company (magnolias are associated with Southern plantations and a dangerously sentimentalized view of the Old South).

The most unsettling section of "Big Boy Leaves Home," the fourth part, brings the implications of its title out into the open: Big Boy will watch in terror as a white mob burns Bobo alive (an atrocity replicated in Jasper, Texas, in 1998, when a white supremacist decapitated a black man by dragging him behind his truck). But first, needing a place to hide until his brother can drive him to Chicago the next morning, Big Boy crawls into a kiln he and his pals had dug. As he does so, he kills a snake that has moved in: "he stomped it with his heel, grinding its head into the dirt" (264), a suggestive echo of Genesis 3:15: "And I [God] will put enmity between thee [Adam] and the woman [Eve], and between thy seed and her seed; it shall bruise thy head, and shalt bruise his heel" (King James Version [hereafter KJV]). As Big Boy waits for Will, he thinks about the good times he and his three friends had while they played in the kiln, but Big Boy also wonders why Bobo does not come. Then he hears two white men who are looking for him; one claims that if Big Boy and Bobo escape, no (white) woman will be safe from black men, all of whom are, presumably, sexual predators. Actually, the charge of rape was often just a ploy to justify the lynching of black men.

A mob then appears with a pillow (for its feathers), a barrel of tar, and gasoline; someone sings, *"We'll hang ever [sic] nigger to a sour apple tree . . ."* (269). As Big Boy watches, the mob finds Bobo and prepares to tar and feather him. Deciding to get souvenirs from this grotesque carnival, the mob takes a finger and then an ear from an apparently still alive Bobo. Hurrying with its horrible task because it is about to rain, the mob pours tar on its soon-to-be-incinerated victim: Big Boy "saw a writhing white mass cradled in yellow flame, and heard screams, one on top of the other, each shriller and shorter than the last" (271). The word "cradled," with its connotations of a mother's love for her child, carries a powerful irony with it. Also ironic is a passage in the story when it begins to rain: one of the white men says he will take some of "yuh ladies" (272) back to town in his car; he is concerned that a "lady" not get wet, but he is indifferent to the heinous acts in which he has just participated. The rain itself suggests a kind of obscene baptism, cleansing the scene of its literal dirt but leaving a far worse kind of dirt untouched. One final irony in Part IV is that man's best friend—a dog accompanying the mob—finds Big Boy in the kiln, but he is able to choke the animal to death before being discovered.

In the concluding section, Big Boy meets up with his brother, Will, who helps him into the truck he is driving to Chicago—the truck that carries Big Boy away from his home.

In his autobiographical *Black Boy*, Wright mentions that this short story poses a question: "What quality of will must a Negro possess to live and die with dignity in a country that denied his humanity?" (402). The answer seems to be that he must possess the kind that Big Boy has, a will that can withstand witnessing horrific violence and terror.

CHARACTER DEVELOPMENT

Character development in the first story of *Uncle Tom's Children* is modest, because what stirs Wright's imagination in the narration is the unspeakable horror of a lynching. Big Boy himself is sketched as a young black man who is forced to become a mature one quickly, if he wants to survive. Instead of being allowed to grow up slowly in a world in which young men can go swimming without being killed for their skin color, he must leave this "home" with the knowledge that it is a racial hell. Before his trip northward, he is characterized as a typical adolescent male, out for a good time with his pals, and noted for his size, strength, and love of verbal combat. He reacts to the murderous white mob with inevitable fear, but also with a strong determination to survive. Of necessity, he changes quickly from a cocky adolescent to a young man who knows all too well how precarious his existence is in a racially divided society.

The white woman in the story, Bertha, acts terrified of the four black teenagers, yet she moves toward their clothes instead of away from them, which suggests her conflicted feelings toward black males and results in their ironically approaching her to retrieve their clothes. Wright may be suggesting that she is fascinated by the myth of black male sexuality without consciously realizing it. While Lester and Buck are characterized as typical teenagers, Bobo is singled out by Wright as a particularly terrible victim of mob violence. Somebody amputates a finger and then an ear while Bobo is presumably still alive. As Big Boy watches, the mob pours tar on Bobo and sets him on fire. The mob's dismemberment of Bobo is a devastating self-indictment of which it is completely unaware.

THEMATIC ISSUES

Although "Big Boy Leaves Home" may skimp on character development, it offers substantial compensation in the form of numerous thematic strands woven throughout the narrative. Without exhausting the thematic possibilities, readers can respond to the following concerns: the process of maturation, the sexuality of black men and white women, and the emptiness of white claims of racial superiority. Big Boy is pushed out of the nest suddenly by white racism. He does not have the luxury of assimilating the experience because his survival depends on his growing up overnight. From an adolescent just having a good time with three friends, Big Boy is transformed into someone who dramatically learns what the cost of merely having black skin can be: being burned alive. The Edenic atmosphere at the beginning of the story does contain a harbinger of a looming postlapsarian world (a world after the fall of humanity)—Lester teases Buck by claiming that his mind is lower than a snake's belly, an allusion to the garden in Genesis from which Eve and Adam were expelled after their encounter with a snake—but Big Boy and his buddies overlook it. Here, however, Wright racializes the biblical tale: for him, the white woman in "Big Boy Leaves Home," Bertha, is the serpent, whereas Big Boy and his pals are prelapsarian Adams. The irony is that the young men are not only not seduced by Bertha, they are terrified of her; but she, interestingly enough, stands next to their clothes, forcing them to approach her. In other words, these four Adams lose their innocence even though they did not cause their own fall, in contrast to what happens in Genesis. If there is a profound disparity between the crime and the punishment in Genesis, it is also a deep one in this story.

Wright is well aware of the sexual mythology vibrating in the background of a story involving black men and a white woman. Many black men have been lynched in the United States because of this myth: it goes without saying, according to the racist fantasy, that if there is sex between a black man and a white woman, it is rape, because no "lady"—that is, no white woman—would voluntarily enter into such a relationship with a black man. The stereotype of the black man as rapist or sexual predator is also under pressure here, as the four young men are considering anything but sex when Bertha sees them naked near her father-in-law's swimming hole; they know that sex with her equals death for them. When black men were historically lynched on a routine basis, a commonplace strategy was simply to ask white men if they cared about the feelings of white women or not, the implication being that if they were really men, they did. Lynching would then serve as the confirmation of their manhood; it would also ensure maintaining the racial status quo. If black men were in fact predisposed to rape white women, it is odd that they did not do so from 1861 to 1865, when many white men were away from their Southern homes, fighting in the Civil War. The myth would have it that black men became predators *after* the war, when white soldiers had returned home. Wright knew better, as "Big Boy Leaves Home" so powerfully demonstrates.

He also knew better than to accept the ludicrous claim of white superiority: what "superior" person would burn an "inferior" alive, just before cutting off body parts as "souvenirs?" And how do assertions of white supremacy stand up, Wright asks in the story, to lynching someone when there has been no investigation of the supposed crime, let alone a public trial? Lynching, of course, assures that there will never be a trial, which is understandable, assuming that a trial contains the potential for revealing that the accused is innocent. A bitter irony in all of this is the fact that lynching did not prevent voluntary sex between black men and white women anyway, which is what white men were really anxious about. In fact, the problem also had to do with white men who wanted to maintain their near sexual monopoly over white women and their access to black women, while denying black men access to white women. The theory of white supremacy comes down to little more than a ploy to justify white male privilege and a strategy to shut down black attempts at equality. Setting someone on fire is a strange way of maintaining superiority.

A STRUCTURALIST READING

Of the many different ways to read a literary work, structuralism provides a particularly useful approach to "Big Boy Leaves Home." Structuralism emphasizes the relations between signifying elements in a text. Structuralist literary theory itself includes several different varieties; the one applied here examines the cultural code that helps to give coherence to a literary text. For instance, the way Janie Crawford, the central character in Zora Neale Hurston's *Their Eyes Were Watching God*, dresses is more than a statement about clothing: it also reveals changes in her attitude. Thus, when she wears overalls, she is signaling a challenge to male privilege. Similarly, in Wright's story, there is a system of signs that can be decoded to reveal a message—in this case, a message regarding sexuality. Even a casual glance at the text of "Big Boy Leaves Home" will take in the following significant items: holes, snakes, swinging sticks, Big Boy's very name, an idyllic setting, a woman, the allure of nature, weapons, the reference to "jelly roll." But where there might have been sex, there is truly horrible violence, a denial of the "natural" order of things.

In a structuralist reading of "Black Boy Leaves Home," the Empress of the Garden is not enticed by a snake, as she is in so many myths about paradise; she *is* the snake. In other words, Bertha is a code word for evil in the story, because her encounter with the four young black men results in the death of three of them. Their sexuality is blocked by death, just as it is blocked in a different way when they cover their genitals as they first see her: confronted by a mythological representation of evil, they conceal their own snakes; unfortunately for them, however, they must nevertheless approach the evil in order to retrieve parts of themselves (here represented as their clothes). For black men, then, Wright's code indicates that a white woman is ruination, just as, according to Genesis, Eve was for Adam. But the God in Wright's garden, the white man, does not punish Bertha; rather, he punishes her victims, four innocent black men, by killing three and banishing one so they will not be threats to white females. What kind of God is this, Wright asks, that punishes victims and protects the source of their downfall?

"DOWN BY THE RIVERSIDE"

PLOT DEVELOPMENT

The second story in *Uncle Tom's Children*, "Down by the Riverside," is comprised of six parts. The plot is driven by the theme of endurance and determination in the face of racial and natural challenges, especially as seen in the main character, a black man named Mann. In contrast to the sentiment expressed in the hymn from which Wright took this title (the speaker is going to lie down his sword and shield down by the riverside), Wright's protagonist never stops fighting.

Part I reveals the source of the threat from nature in this tale as an out-of-control Mississippi River (one of the worst floods involving the Mississippi occurred in 1927, which may be the basis for the story). With no provisions in his house and a pregnant wife, Lulu, whose hips are too narrow for the birth of the baby, Mann must get his family to food and his wife to a doctor. Mann's brother-in-law, Bob Cobb, arrives at Mann's house with a white boat he has stolen from the white postmaster, Henry Heartfield (who, unlike Mann, is not filled with heart). Mann announces that he is going to take Lulu to the Red Cross Hospital in Heartfield's boat, even though anyone who sees him will surely be able to identify the boat as Heartfield's. To add to Mann's problems, Cobb tells him that there are armed white men in town and that a rumor is afloat that 23 black people have already been killed trying to run away from forced labor on the levee. Undeterred, Mann puts a pistol in his pocket and, after the family sings the song that is the source of the story's title, rows off with his family—his wife Lulu, his son Peewee, and his mother-in-law Grannie.

In Part II, Mann rows against a strong current to a house along the riverbank to ask if there is a phone he can use; but the house—in the first of several coincidences that structure the plot—turns out to be that of the Heartfields. After Henry Heartfield fires four shots at Mann because he recognizes the boat as his own stolen property, Mann shoots and kills him. Although he is tempted to give up on his mission, Mann rows on: "Ahm goin on, no mattah *whut*." (293). He then encounters two soldiers, one of whom thinks it is funny that Mann has rowed against such a current. The soldiers call for a motorboat, which, when Mann's boat is hitched to it, tows him and his family to the hospital, where a white doctor soon informs Mann that his wife is dead.

To further reinforce his theme of the endurance of the black community in the face of white racism and natural disasters, Wright presents us in Part III with a white colonel who is stationed at the hospital and is totally indifferent to Mann's recent loss of his wife (and the unborn child within her). The colonel will not even allow Mann to go back to the hills with Grannie and Peewee; instead, he orders Mann to work on the levee. But it does not hold after Mann arrives, so he and a young black man named Brinkley are assigned a boat, in Part IV, and ordered to the Red Cross Hospital, where they can rescue people from the rising Mississippi and take them to the hills. Noble and heroic to the end, Wright's protagonist, along with Brinkley, helps people leave the hospital safely, and then they are given a piece of paper with the address of a family that badly needs help written on it. In another straining of credibility, the family turns out to be the Heartfields.

When, in Part V, Brinkley and Mann find Mrs. Heartfield and her two children still alive, her son Ralph recognizes Mann as his father's murderer. As Mann is about to kill Ralph with an axe, the Heartfields' house suddenly tilts in the floodwater (Wright might have been uncomfortable at the thought of Mann killing a child, no matter how understandable the circumstances). Mann, perhaps impossibly high-minded, then helps the Heartfields into the motorboat.

In Part VI, the evidently ungrateful Ralph identifies Mann as his father's killer, and four white soldiers consequently arrest him. Brought before a general and charged with looting and murder, Mann refuses to divulge where he got the Heartfields' boat in order to protect his brother-in-law. The four soldiers take Mann away to execute him, but he tries to escape and is shot repeatedly.

CHARACTER DEVELOPMENT

The character in "Down by the Riverside" who is most developed is the protagonist, Mann, whom Wright constructs as an emblem of the enduring black community, as well as a reaction against Harriet Beecher Stowe's passive figure, Uncle Tom. Mann, on the contrary, acts: he kills a man and almost kills a white child in his attempts to secure the safety of his loved ones; he persists in this goal when faced with practically insurmountable obstacles; and he refuses to betray his brother-in-law at the expense of his own life. Even if he is unbelievably noble, he is a distillation of the best the black community has to offer: a brave, determined, and strong-minded individual, unquestionably devoted to his family. He is a successful embodiment of Wright's major themes in the story itself—and the near opposite of the author's own father.

Wright characterizes Lulu, Mann's pregnant wife, as a passive sufferer, in that she dies before she can even give birth to a new member of her community, a birth that is precarious in its own right due to her seeming powerlessness (i.e., her too-narrow hips). One light note is provided in the character of the young black man Brinkley, who is cast heroically, in that he is especially adept at handling the motorboat he and Mann use to rescue the Heartfields. In contrast, Wright characterizes the patriarch of that family, Henry Heartfield, as a particularly vicious racist, as heartless as he is bigoted.

THEMATIC ISSUES

Hovering over the entirety of "Down by the Riverside" is the theme of self-determination and perseverance, even in the face of the most formidable adverse forces. Mann resists to his utmost strength a horrible white racism and its equivalent in nature, an immense river that has overflowed its banks. Like Sisyphus, the mythological figure who had to keep rolling a rock up a hill only to watch it roll back down again, Mann never gives up; his strength comes from within himself, his family, and the black community, especially the black church. Readers who are embarrassed at Wright's doubts regarding the black community, as expressed in the notorious passage early in Chapter 2 of *Black Boy*, should reconsider his position on it in light of this story. As a man of the folk, Mann is a black folk hero, the epitome of dignity and integrity, the incarnation of black manhood. Not to be overlooked, too, is his devotion to his family.

A FEMINIST READING

Of the many different types of feminist literary criticism, a particularly useful kind in the case of "Down by the Riverside" looks for omissions of, as well as representations of, women in literary works. The name of the male protagonist in this story goes far in suggesting Wright's gender-based assumptions. A man performs heroic tasks; women, especially black women, are passive sufferers: they have children, or die from complications resulting from pregnancy, or suffer in silence. What they do not do in life, or in "Down by the Riverside," is rescue people from floods, or handle motorboats well (as the male Brinkley does), or kill people when necessary (as Mann does in the case of Henry Heartfield); these are a man's jobs. Such thinking not only defines heroism in narrowly patriarchal terms, but it also suppresses the fact that heroic accomplishments are often enabled by someone other than the hero: the women taking care of children, preparing the meals, and generally keeping to the background. Reading "Down by the Riverside" in this manner denigrates neither Wright's nor Mann's achievements, but it does clarify them.

"LONG BLACK SONG"

PLOT DEVELOPMENT

In the third short story of *Uncle Tom's Children*, Wright structures the narrative around the visit of a white traveling salesman to the home of Sarah, a young black woman caring for Ruth, her newborn. The effects of the visit include the whipping and possible death of the salesman, the death of Sarah's husband, the death of several other men, and the burning down of Sarah's house. Part I opens with Wright making it clear that Sarah is very lonely because Silas, her husband, has been gone a week. Furthermore, she pines for a former boyfriend, Tom, who has not yet returned from fighting in World War I, which has ended, thus placing the time of the story at around 1918–1919. The traveling salesman, never named, drives up, learns that Sarah's husband is away, and tries to sell her a combination clock-graphophone (a device for recording and reproducing sounds on wax records). After a little time passes, he forces her to have sex with him. As if paying for services rendered, the salesman tells Sarah that she can buy the clock-graphophone for $40, instead of the original asking price of $50.

The next morning, Silas returns home with some red cloth and some high-top shoes for his wife. He proudly tells her that he has bought ten more acres of land with the $250 he was paid for his cotton. In other words, in emulating the whites, Silas has turned his life into a series of financial and material transactions, and in so doing, he is not as different from the salesman as he might think he is. Noting the clock-graphophone in their bedroom, Silas asks Sarah if the salesman was white. He becomes angry when he observes that although it is marked for sale at $50, Sarah had told him she paid only $40. After heaving it out the front door, he angrily accuses Sarah of lying about how much it cost. It is at this point in the plot that Wright stretches credibility by having Silas notice a yellow pencil left in the house by the salesman and by having him discover a damp handkerchief in their bedroom.

Without even asking what happened, Silas takes Sarah to the barn to whip her, but she runs away, worried that she has left Ruth in the house unattended. After getting the baby, Sarah decides to take her to a relative's house. The narrator then remarks that she "was sorry for what she had done. Silas was as good to her as any black man could be to a black woman" (347), an ambiguous observation that could mean one of two things: black men are not all that good to black women, but given that, Silas was comparatively good to her, or he was as good to her as a man can be. Like many other women, Sarah has been socialized to assume that crises are all her fault.

As the story proceeds, the salesman returns, accompanied by another white man, and Silas whips him and kills one of them (it is not clear which one) with his rifle. The plot concludes with a mob of whites setting the couple's house on fire while Silas is in it, shooting back at them; as Sarah watches, her husband is burned alive in the house that was so important to him.

CHARACTER DEVELOPMENT

Wright depicts Sarah (which means "princess" in Hebrew) as an innocent victim of an old story: a white male sexual predator takes advantage of a defenseless woman. But in a twist on the old pattern, Silas does get revenge on the transgressor. Sarah tries to be the best wife and mother she can be to Silas and Ruth, but because of something beyond her control, sexual exploitation by a more powerful male, she is victimized twice, in the second instance by a husband who reacts to her first victimization without any understanding of it whatsoever; in fact, he makes no effort to understand. He has internalized capitalistic values to the point that he thinks of his wife in the same way that he thinks of his house or his land—as commodities that he, and he alone, owns. Possession and ownership equal masculinity, in his system of values, so the salesman trespassed on Silas's property when he had sexual intercourse with Sarah. What Sarah thinks of all this, let alone concern for his daughter, plays no role at all in Silas's reaction to his wife's experience. The salesman himself is characterized as nothing but an opportunist who thinks that his status as a white male allows him access to Sarah if he so desires it.

THEMATIC ISSUES

Wright addresses several themes in "Long Black Song," including the issue of capitalism versus preindustrialism. Silas and the salesman view people, land, crops, anything, as commodities with fluctuating market values. Silas assumes that if he emulates white material values, he will be fulfilled; the story's ending suggests otherwise. Perhaps the clearest indication of the difference in the two sets of values involves an assumption Sarah relates: clocks are not necessary to her because she tells time by nature's rhythms; for Silas and the salesman, however, time must be calibrated carefully because it is another form of capital.

Clearly related to this theme is the opposition Wright establishes between technology and nature. Sarah, for example, lives in harmony with nature without trying to control it; but to the salesman, nature is a force to be explained and understood in scientific terms. Sarah finds it amusing that he is studying science, which he defines as "why things are as they are" (336). The clock-graphophone contraption itself suggests the intrusion of twentieth-century technology into a natural way of life, just as the salesman's car contrasts with Silas's traditional farmwagon.

A GENDERED READING

Gendered readings of literary works take into account perspectives of both women and men. Rather than assuming, in other words, that an interpretation of "Long Black Song" from Silas's point of view is universal, a gendered reading would accommodate his vantage point *and* his wife's. From the former's point of view, the rape of Sarah is an insult to him as a property owner, as he thinks of her as his possession. Someone cannot use someone else's property unless given permission to do so, and Silas did not give the salesman permission to "use" his wife.

Sarah's feelings about being raped are never given expression by Wright or considered by her husband; she is on her own where that is concerned. Her feelings are of no consequence to her husband (or to the author apparently), because it is the feelings of men that matter here. But from Sarah's viewpoint, being treated like nothing but sexual prey by a stranger is no doubt utterly callous and reprehensible. Sarah, then, has to put aside her own feelings while trying to deal with those of an outraged and humiliated husband, who is determined to kill or be killed, even though that will leave his daughter and wife on their own. Sarah evidently thinks it goes without saying that a man's feelings take precedence over a woman's, and thus she never challenges her husband's obsession with seeking revenge on the rapist. When Silas's sense of masculinity is threatened, he believes anything goes to settle the score. He gives no thought to why the rape might have occurred, how his wife views it, or whether there are alternatives to violence. *He* is extremely upset; therefore, there is nothing else to consider.

From a gendered perspective, though, there is plenty more to consider, particularly the violation of Sarah's body and how she feels about that. If Silas had loved his wife as much as himself, the violent conclusion to "Long Black Song" could have been replaced with understanding and even a strengthened marriage: revenge is not the inevitable outcome of rape, but Silas thinks otherwise.

"FIRE AND CLOUD"

PLOT DEVELOPMENT

The plot of the fourth story in *Uncle Tom's Children* unfolds in a straightforward way, from the opening concern about Dan Taylor's congregation's lack of food to the march for it at the end of the story. The fulcrum for the plot is the issue of whether or not Taylor will support the march, which is to be made up of poor whites and blacks. Because the white relief in town will not give blacks any food, Taylor sends a committee of ten men and women from his church to meet with Mayor Bolton, but they get nowhere.

In the meantime, Taylor confronts stress from four sources: first, Mayor Bolton, Chief of Police Bruden, and the head of the "industrial Squad," Mr. Lowe; second, his own son Jimmy and his friends; third, the members of his church; and fourth, Hadley and Green, two Communists. The first group wants Taylor to keep the black community from marching. The second wants to resist white domination through violence, which could get all the black people in the community killed. The third group is desperate for a solution to the lack of food in the black community. Finally, the fourth wants Taylor to allow the use of his name on leaflets that could help bring out a large crowd of demonstrators whom the police would thus be forced to treat with respect; he refuses.

In his meeting with the three powerful white men, Taylor informs them that black people are so hungry that they are going to march no matter what he tells them. As they leave his house, they threaten him and demand that he stop the march. Then Taylor promises the deacons of his church that he will support the march if they will and that if his congregation marches in the morning, he will be with them.

The incident that precipitates Taylor's total commitment to the march is his being assaulted at night by three white men, who drive off with him in their car and tie him to a tree. As he recites the Lord's Prayer, they whip him until he lapses into unconsciousness. Upon regaining consciousness, Taylor manages to make it to his church, where Jimmy relates to him that Hadley and Green are saying that he ran out on them and that Deacon Smith got the board to vote him out of his church. Soon afterward, Taylor tells his congregation that he has had a revelation: cooperating with the whites was a mistake because they granted him favors in order to control the black community through him. At that, he and the crowd, joined by poor whites, march into town. As they arrive, a policeman tells Taylor that Mayor Bolton wants to see him up in front of the marchers, but Taylor says he will see him back in the crowd. When the mayor hurries toward Taylor, the latter informs him that he, the mayor, will tell the crowd that food will be provided if everyone will just go home peacefully. This is when Taylor realizes that freedom belongs to the strong, that is, to unified groups of people.

CHARACTER DEVELOPMENT

Of the numerous characters in "Fire and Cloud," Dan Taylor is the most fully developed. A man of goodwill and a leader in his community as the pastor of his church, Taylor is a prototypical characterization of Martin Luther King Jr. who grows into understanding that the future of his community lies in organization and unification. Whereas before his revelation Taylor had unthinkingly accepted favors from influential whites who then, of course, expected his "cooperation" in return, he comes to understand that he cannot be a genuine leader in the black community so long as he allows himself to be bought off by powerful whites. He also grows into the realization that Christianity and Marxism may be compatible for political purposes, as when his congregation and poor whites join together at least to march for relief from starvation: social class can trump race on occasion.

In terms of the other main players, Taylor's oldest son, Jimmy, is characterized as a more militant agitator for racial justice. He favors the use of violence to oppose white privilege, but his father knows well that this strategy could prove fatal to the black community. Wright paints Deacon Smith as a traitor who will sell out any member of the black community at the slightest opportunity to do so. The three white political leaders are developed in terms of the degree of their readiness to turn to violence to repress the blacks: Mayor Bolton prefers political manipulation, Chief of Police Bruden, the law, and Mr. Lowe, as his name suggests, brute force.

THEMATIC ISSUES

Wright's thematic concerns in "Fire and Cloud" include the value of black solidarity and unity (whereas the first three stories in the collection examine the reactions of relatively isolated black individuals to social pressure) and the central importance of the black church. So long as Dan Taylor engages in personal accommodations with Mayor Bolton and his white friends, he will not be a political threat, but once he stops striking individual deals and joins with the mass of black people in town, Taylor seriously threatens the status quo. "Fire and Cloud" emphasizes the importance of black people sticking together to resist external (the white community) and internal (the traitor Deacon Smith) threats. Going a racial step further and joining forces with the poor whites may be a violation of historical reality, but it does serve as a model for what could happen.

What mobilizes and organizes the communal energy in the story is the black church, which receives more respectful attention here than in *Black Boy*. The story's title itself echoes an old hymn, as well as Exodus 40:38: "For the cloud of the Lord was upon the tabernacle by day, and fire was on it by night, in the sight of all the house of Israel, throughout all their journeys" (KJV). As a modern-day Moses, Taylor stands on a religious foundation, the black church, to initiate social and racial changes, much like Martin Luther King Jr. did in the 1960s.

A MARXIST READING

"Fire and Cloud" invites a Marxist reading because it is written from a Marxist perspective, at a time before Wright developed doubts about communism. Marx emphasized that social class is the ultimate determinant of an individual's experience, and that is indeed the case here, as long as one assumes that race can be incorporated into social class, as Wright does in this story. Working-class blacks and whites, in joining together, are able to gain at least some leverage over the ruling whites; Wright and Marx see such class solidarity as the key element in a social and political revolution. Dan Taylor's consciousness is transformed from a traditional Christian point of view to a more militant, secular one that understands the need for aggressive social action in the face of intransigent white prerogatives, as represented by Mayor Bolton and Chief of Police Bruden. Although there are two Communists in the story, Hadley and Green, it is the black community itself, along with Taylor, that is responsible for resisting white privileges and demanding that people's basic needs be met.

"BRIGHT AND MORNING STAR"

PLOT DEVELOPMENT

The plot of the last story in *Uncle Tom's Children*, "Bright and Morning Star," a story that was added for the 1940 edition, develops linearly from beginning to end, with mounting tension generated mainly by the question of whether or not the central character, An Sue, will be able to prevent a traitor from revealing the names of the members of the local Communist group to the town sheriff. A black woman of strong Christian faith, Sue awaits the return of one of her two sons, Johnny-Boy, from organizing a local Communist group; her other son, Sug, is in jail for the same activity. Johnny-Boy's white girlfriend, Reva, comes to Sue's cabin to let her know that the sheriff came to see Reva's father about a possible Communist Party meeting, so someone must tell the other party members the meeting has been canceled. It is also apparent that someone informed the sheriff about the meeting in the first place. Reva devises a plan to send Johnny-Boy to talk to all the party members, warning them to stay away from her father's house, which the sheriff is watching.

After Reva leaves Sue's, Johnny-Boy comes home; he and his mother argue over whether or not it was a white person who revealed to the authorities that there was going to be a meeting at Reva's father's place. Johnny-Boy takes the orthodox Communist position that he does not see race as the pertinent issue, but only the class distinction between rich and poor. After Johnny-Boy departs to carry out Reva's plan, the sheriff and some other white men forcibly enter An Sue's house while she is in bed. Instead of getting out of her house, as she insists, the sheriff slaps her, hits her in the face with his fist, and kicks her in the face and stomach. The traitor in the plot, a white man named Booker (named after Booker T. Washington, regarded by some as a traitor to the black community, who died in 1915), arrives after the men have left to tell An Sue that the sheriff is holding her son at Foley's Woods in an effort to make him identify other party members. Booker also explains to her that Johnny-Boy was apprehended before he had a chance to warn his fellow members about what has been happening; as such, she will need to tell him who they are so that he can warn them himself. Out of confusion and disorientation, Sue complies, despite her suspicions about Booker's integrity. Booker then leaves her cabin, of course intending to pass the names on to the sheriff.

At her father's request, Reva returns to Sue's cabin and tells her to beware of Booker because he is an informer. Sue immediately realizes that Booker is certainly en route to Foley's Woods to give the sheriff the names, but Booker is unaware of a shortcut she knows. Accordingly, after Reva retires, Sue gets Johnny-Boy's gun, conceals it in a bedsheet, and heads off to Foley's Woods. When she arrives, she does not shoot the men she discovers torturing her son, for she is focused on killing Booker before he can reveal the names. Hence, she is forced to watch while her son's kneecaps are broken with a crowbar and both his eardrums are smashed, deafening him. An Sue does manage to shoot Booker, but her son is then killed, as is she, but not before experiencing satisfaction in knowing that she prevented Booker from betraying party members.

CHARACTER DEVELOPMENT

Character development in "Bright and Morning Star" concentrates on An Sue and her son Johnny-Boy, who disagree over religion and over whether or not blacks can trust whites. Sue, correctly as it turns out, is deeply skeptical about her son's contention that she should see poor and rich, not black and white, as the distinction between people, but her view is complicated by the fact that a young white woman whom Sue does trust, Reva (suggesting revelation, revolution), loves Johnny-Boy. On the other hand, Sue is more than justified in her distrust of Booker, the white informer, which suggests that her son may be a naive Marxist in that he thinks social class always trumps race. Their disagreement about religion may not be as deep as first appears, for Johnny-Boy, while accepting Marx as his savior, does not realize that even as he rejects his mother's religion, he simultaneously embraces a secular version of it. For her part, Sue deifies Johnny-Boy, the bright and shining star of the title, which is referred to in a Protestant hymn, as well as in the books of the Song of Solomon and Revelation in the Christian Bible. The only other significant character, the sheriff, Wright develops into a monster of vicious racial oppression.

THEMATIC ISSUES

Several thematic issues inform the last story in *Uncle Tom's Children*: in particular, positive treatment of a black woman and her family and communism. In contrast to some other depictions of black women in Wright's work, including those in *Black Boy* and *Native Son*, An Sue is portrayed in a very affirmative manner. She would do anything for her two sons, except betray others (it is tempting to compare her to Sethe in Toni Morrison's *Beloved*, a mother who takes her own daughter's life because she thinks letting her grow up to be a slave would be worse than killing her). An Sue is fully aware of Johnny-Boy's suffering as he is being tortured, but she believes it is better to let the torture continue than to put an end to his physical pain and thereby get herself killed before she can stop Booker's plan to reveal the names of the other Communists. In other words, as much as she loves Johnny-Boy, she is willing to tolerate his brutalization a little longer to prevent a worse evil, the betrayal of her compatriots. Here is a celebration of a noble woman who could be classified as a black peasant, a social category that makes Wright uneasy in his autobiography, and here is a celebration also of a black family in which violence has not replaced love, as it has in the families in *Black Boy* and *Native Son*.

Related to this theme is the central political theory in "Bright and Morning Star," communism, an ideology that regards social class as a far greater historical determinant than race: what keeps people from universal equality is social class, not skin color. This is certainly Johnny-Boy's view, but African American experience suggests otherwise, for it indicates that in the United States, at least until very recently, race overrides social class. An Sue grasps this point firmly, whereas Johnny-Boy refuses to, which contributes to his being seized, tortured, and killed by whites, even though he was trying to help white *and* black people move toward a political revolution that would benefit both in his judgment.

AN ALLEGORICAL READING

An allegory is a literary device that uses symbols to represent truths about human existence. Plato's allegory of the cave is probably the most famous example: in it, Socrates, Plato's speaker, talks about people in a cave to make the point that everyday reality is an imitation of what is called an "Ideal Reality." The beds we sleep in, for instance, are inferior imitations of an ideal bed that exists outside of ordinary reality. So in "Bright and Morning Star," Wright has written a short story about the plight of one particular black mother and her son that can also be interpreted as an allegory of social struggle for a great number of people. The title suggests hope and illumination, as does the beacon light referred to throughout the story: even in darkness, literal or figurative, there is hope. Some of the characters' names can also be taken allegorically:

Booker, as mentioned earlier, reminds us of Booker T. Washington, considered a black traitor by some people. And the name "Reva," as was also suggested, hints at revelation or revolution, in another allegorical gesture by Wright. While An Sue's name is not allegorical, as a character she can be taken as a representation of any black mother who has loved her children more than herself. Lastly, the torturing of Johnny-Boy symbolizes what has been done to black men throughout the history of the United States, with the sheriff as a singular emblem of unconstrained racist authority.

Native Son
(1940, 1991)

Sixty years after its first publication, *Native Son* remains Richard Wright's most powerful and most frequently discussed novel. A carefully written and constructed work, it revolves around its protagonist, Bigger Thomas, a 20-year-old black man who murders two women: Mary Dalton, the daughter of his employer, and Bessie Mears, his girlfriend. Wright suggests that this violence is one of the effects of 350 years of slavery and oppression; Bigger Thomas is a native son of the United States. And yet, to many readers, he is more than a victim: he is a black man insisting that his violent acts have significance. (What that significance is has been the subject of considerable and ongoing debate.) Wright's most powerful creation is hard to pin down and may not have been fully understood by the author himself, let alone the readers of the novel.

What is clear, however, is that the primary cause of Bigger's nightmarish experience is white racism. Wright argues: if the whites in *Native Son* had recognized that Bigger is a human being rather than a stereotyped figment of their imaginations, he would not have become a killer. Put another way, *Native Son* is deeply concerned with the issue of moral responsibility—Bigger Thomases do not just appear; they are products of sociological conditions, which is not to say that they are mere automatons, but that they cannot be held totally responsible for their bitter anger and resentment. Part of Wright's achievement here, then, is helping us understand the forces that create a brutal and violent man.

But there is considerably more to Wright's most famous novel than Bigger Thomas as a product of white racism. As a detective novel, it provides us with a generous supply of excitement as we wonder whether or not Bigger will be caught by the Chicago police. It also offers us a compelling literary experience in its depiction of a major American city in the wintertime; in fact, Chicago might be considered a prominent character in *Native Son*. In addition, the relationship between black women and black men receives substantial treatment, with results that have not always been flattering to Richard Wright. Of particular interest to contemporary readers is the novel's examination of how the media—particularly newspapers and movies—figure in the world of Bigger Thomas.

PLOT DEVELOPMENT

Divided into three named books ("Fear," "Flight," and "Fate"), the plot of *Native Son* is constituted by the circumstances that made Bigger Thomas who he is and by what he therefore represents in a larger societal context. "Fear" is intensely exciting and suspenseful as Bigger begins and ends a 24-hour period in his life with violence: soon after getting up in the morning, he pounds a rat's head in with a shoe; and later that night, he smothers and then decapitates the daughter of his new employer. Since racism is "in the head," a mental state, it is suggestive that he consistently attacks the heads of his victims (he will later smash in his girlfriend's head with a brick). After he dangles the dead rat in his sister's face, which causes her to faint, Mrs. Thomas, Bigger's mother, tells him she sometimes wonders why she gave birth to him. She also claims that if he had any "manhood" in him, the family would not have to live amid a garbage dump. Wright seems to suggest here, then, that part of what has made Bigger a resentful, bitter, young black man is the black woman, based on this opening scene. If Mrs. Thomas had not construed manhood in the narrow sense of only the ability to make money, then it is implied that Bigger would not have felt so strongly his perceived lack of worth.

When Bigger leaves his mother's one-room tenement apartment, we see more of the social environment that Wright indicts for producing such young men: Bigger loiters on a street with Gus, a member of his gang, before the two go to Doc's poolroom to plan the robbery of a delicatessen. To conceal his fear of robbing a white man, Bigger provokes Gus into a fight, which results in the gang's not robbing the deli, which was Bigger's intent all along. It is late in the afternoon when Bigger makes his fateful visit to the home of Mr. Dalton, for whom he has agreed to become the family chauffeur, because the Thomases will be denied welfare if he does not. The Daltons' house is alien territory for Bigger, containing as it does modernist paintings, a sense of tranquility, and most important, Mr. Dalton's daughter, Mary, who represents to Bigger all that he is not supposed to have—wealth, privilege, white sexuality. In one of the plot's most powerful ironies, Bigger agrees with Mr. Dalton during his job interview that the two do not anticipate any trouble in Bigger working for him. But the plot devices make it overwhelmingly clear that Mr. Dalton and Bigger will have catastrophic trouble with each other.

Bigger's first job as the Daltons' chauffeur is to drive Mary to the university, but once in the car, she directs him instead to take her to the headquarters of the local Communist Party chapter, where she meets her boyfriend, Jan Erlone. Jan and Mary make the profound mistake of treating someone who is terrified of whites as an equal, particularly when they insist that they go with Bigger to a restaurant black people frequent. Mary finds it stimulating to pretend to fit into black culture, yet she and Jan can easily move back into the safety of the white world at any time simply by returning to the car. The narration throughout this episode indicates that Bigger does not understand whites and that they certainly do not understand him. The ultimate result of this mutual ignorance will be the deaths of Mary Dalton, Bessie Mears, and Bigger Thomas himself.

Wright then structures his plot so as to replicate the famous scene in William Shakespeare's tragedy *Othello*, where the black hero smothers his white wife in her bedroom. After Bigger drops Jan off at a streetcar stop, he takes Mary home, but she is so drunk that he must help her into the house. He eventually manages to get her up to her bedroom, but he is extremely frightened when the blind Mrs. Dalton approaches her daughter's room, checking to see if she is home yet. To keep Mary from mumbling and giving away his presence in her bedroom, Bigger puts a pillow over her face and pushes down hard. Her mother hears some movement and faint mumblings, but when she reaches the bed and smells liquor, she leaves the room disgusted. Bigger initially feels immense relief—until he realizes that Mary is dead. (Interestingly, he will later not want to acknowledge that he did not intend to kill Mary, in order to claim value for the act.)

In panic and fear, Bigger devises an alibi: Jan came home with him and Mary, and Bigger simply left Mary and Jan together in the car when he left for home after work. Bigger then decides that he must get rid of Mary's body and opts to incinerate her corpse in the basement furnace. But the furnace will not accommodate the entire length of her body, so Bigger whacks off Mary's head with a hatchet he finds in the basement. Although this development in the plot sounds sensationalistic, it is actually justified by Wright's primary thematic concerns of depicting the society that produced Bigger and the role he subsequently plays in that society: the United States is creating some extremely violent black men because of its racial ignorance and hatred, the book makes clear.

The plot of Book Two, "Flight," is driven in large part by the question of whether or not Bigger will be caught and by Wright's ongoing thematic intentions. Awaking the next morning in his mother's apartment, he reflects on the previous night: "The thought of what he had done, the awful horror of it, the daring associated with such actions, formed for him for the first time in his fear-ridden life a barrier of protection between him and a world he feared. He had murdered and created a new life for himself" (118–19). Part of the horror of Bigger's life is that he feels reborn through an act of homicidal violence: what, Wright asks, does this suggest about the majority society that hems in Bigger? It is also evident that Bigger is now determined to deny the accidental nature of the crime, because if he accepts that it was not intentional, he undermines the value of the act to him, as a person with will and autonomy. (In one sense, the murder of Mary Dalton can be read as nonaccidental, for in his imagination, Bigger had killed whites many times.)

With his confidence high, Bigger decides to fool the Daltons into believing that their incinerated daughter has been kidnapped in order to extort $10,000 from them. As part of this scheme, he buys an envelope, a pencil, and a flashlight. He also selects an abandoned building in which he and Bessie, whom he has intimidated into joining him in the extortion plot, can hide while waiting to see where and when Mr. Dalton drops off the ransom money. Bigger concludes his ransom note with the words "Do what this letter say" (203); the faulty grammar could have drawn suspicion to Bigger as a speaker of black English, but it does not because the whites cannot conceive of a black man who would be bold enough to kidnap a rich white woman. His giddiness at writing the ransom note is toned down when he grudgingly admits to Bessie that he did kill Mary. To his "All right. They white folks. They done killed plenty of us," she replies, "That don't make it right" (204). Bigger's thinking has been so twisted by his experiences in white America that he would like to believe that this accidental murder is an act of heroism; a number of readers of *Native Son* have agreed with him.

Bigger must soon relinquish his grand ransom scheme because he is quickly exposed as the killer of Mary Dalton. At the Dalton house for work, he discovers that one of the newspaper reporters following the story of Mary's disappearance has found some small pieces of bone and an earring in the ashes of the Dalton furnace. Bigger flees just as the reporters and the authorities realize that Mary has been incinerated in her own home.

Afraid Bessie will crack under pressure from the police when they locate her, Bigger plans to kill her and thus takes her to the abandoned building. At no other point in *Native Son* does Bigger appear more monstrous than in the horrible and graphically described scene in which he smashes Bessie's head in with a brick. Wright implies that a large measure of moral responsibility for the second murder, as well as the first, must be placed on white Americans. A particularly bitter racial irony in the murder of Bessie is that Bigger rapes her before he kills her, something he did not do to Mary. At his trial, the whites assume he raped Mary; but the lack of physical evidence that would have proved them wrong was destroyed when Bigger disposed of her body. Furthermore, that Bigger finds the two murders the most exhilarating acts of his life is a profound indictment of both him and the mainstream society that excluded him.

The end of Book Two maintains intense excitement in the reader, as 8,000 armed white men close in on Bigger at his hideaway. Chased to the top of a water tank on the building's roof, Bigger is able to ward off tear gas and a man who attempts to climb the tank's ladder, but he is unable to withstand the tremendous pressure of a water hose, which blasts him off the tank. He is then dragged out of the apartment building and taken to various police stations.

The plot of Book Three, "Fate," is built upon four major scenes: Bigger's meeting with nearly every character in *Native Son*; his meeting with the new character Boris Max, his attorney; his trial; and his last meeting with Max, just before his execution. Throughout Book Three, Bigger is determined to find positive significance in the murders, no matter what anyone else thinks. In the initial scene, Reverend Hammond, the pastor of Mrs. Thomas's church, is the first in a long series of visitors to the room where Bigger is being held: his offer of repentance to Bigger is rejected because Bigger wants salvation in this world, not the next. Jan enters next, telling Bigger that he is not angry at him: "it's your right to hate me, Bigger. I see now that you couldn't do anything else but that; it was all you had" (332). However implausible this remark, coming as it does from a man who has just lost the woman he loves at the hands of Bigger, it also serves as evidence that *Native Son* is not antiwhite, which may have been Wright's intention.

Into Bigger's increasingly crowded room next come Boris Max and Buckley, the state's attorney, who argue about whether Bigger is worth defending: in many ways, this is a key issue in the novel, with Buckley arguing against Bigger's worthiness and Max arguing in favor of it. Buckley, largely because he is running for reelection as state's attorney, claims that Bigger is a subhuman monster, but Max says he is a product of a society that refuses to grant him human status. As the plot unfolds early in Book Three, the rape and murder of the black Bessie Mears is never cited: it goes without saying that she does not matter.

After Mrs. Thomas is admitted to the room, Bigger's sister and brother, Vera and Buddy, followed by Jack, G. H., and Gus, the members of Bigger's gang, trail in. Bigger feels that they ought to be glad about what he did. Wright may be suggesting that Bigger is so brutalized by his environment that he takes pleasure in killing. Eventually, everyone but Buckley leaves the room, and while Buckley elicits a confession from Bigger, Bigger does make it clear that he alone committed the crime: this is something that Bigger Thomas, a black man, did.

Back in his jail cell after an inquest, Bigger is visited by his attorney, Boris Max, whom he tells it does not matter whether he dies in hope or in despair; yet the narrator indicates that Bigger knows it does matter a great deal to him. Although unable to explain why he killed Mary, Bigger reacts strongly when Max asks him if he liked her: he exclaims that he hated her, even though he was sexually attracted to her the night of the murder. He also acknowledges that he was never in love with anybody in his life and that he killed Bessie to save himself. Bigger represents violent defiance of white contempt for black people. As he explains to Max in this interview, whites have excluded him from almost everything, but they cannot take away the fact that he killed two women, especially a privileged white one. By the end of this encounter, Bigger is, incredibly for some readers, very tempted to believe in the idea that blacks and whites are equally human; if that is the case, then he has been blind, too, in that he does not view white people as individual human beings but more as a kind of collective oppositional natural force, like an earthquake or a flood.

The third high point of the plot of Book Three is Bigger's trial, which takes place before a judge only, because Max knows his client would have no chance whatsoever before a white jury. In his introductory statement, Max takes the position that Bigger is a social symbol, produced by a racist system. Noting that for powerful whites such as Buckley, Bigger presents an opportunity for exploitation to serve their own interests, Max believes that there is an even deeper problem: the enslavement of black people and the horrible effects it has produced, including guilt, hatred, and fear in the white community. If Wright endorses Max's speech, then Max may be telling us what the first two books have shown us. He goes on to say to the judge that if Bigger Thomas is multiplied 12 million times, "allowing for environmental and temperamental variations, and for those Negroes who are completely under the influence of the church, you have the psychology of the Negro people" (463). In other words, Bigger is a warning of an impending racial holocaust. Max pleads with the judge that Bigger be given a life sentence instead of a death sentence, but Buckley insists on the death penalty, as that is the only way to ensure that white people can sleep at night again after what Bigger has done. Pandering strongly to the most debased stereotypes about black men and white women, Buckley argues that Bigger burned Mary's corpse to conceal evidence of crimes even worse than rape: "That treacherous beast must have known that if the marks of his teeth were ever seen on the innocent white flesh of her breasts, he would not have been accorded the high honor of sitting here in this court of law" (480). Buckley takes advantage of the very prejudices against black people that Max points out led to the two murders in the first place. The judge finds in Buckley's favor.

The plot concludes with the protagonist's attempt to prepare himself for his execution. Bigger wants to see Max once more in order to regain the intense feelings of vitality and self-worth he experienced when he talked about his crimes with Max earlier. As frustrated as he is, Bigger is nevertheless determined to convey to Max what he feels, but Max is terrified when Bigger claims that what he killed for, he is. That is, Bigger killed to live—an idea that Max is unable to face, even when he tells Bigger good-bye for the last time. A steel door clangs shut as Max leaves, just as an alarm clock clanged at the beginning of *Native Son*. This last turn of the plot remains controversial, with some readers arguing that the Bigger we see just before his execution is a tragic figure, and other readers countering that a man who smothers one woman to escape detection in her bedroom and smashes in the head of another woman with a brick to shut her up is anything but tragic.

CHARACTER DEVELOPMENT

All the characters in *Native Son* function to develop Wright's two themes of what produced Bigger Thomas and what Bigger Thomas means. His fatherless family, for instance, lives in a one-room, rat-infested tenement apartment, in a building owned by Mr. Dalton, incidentally. Comprised of Mrs. Thomas and her two other children, Vera and Buddy, Bigger's family has no privacy, little money, and less hope. Mrs. Thomas puts her faith into a religion that promises happiness in another world but that does not solve Bigger's problems in this one. Wondering sometimes why she gave birth to her oldest son, she tells him that the family would not have to live in such grim circumstances if he were truly a man. By equating masculinity with money, Bigger's mother has emasculated him, Wright suggests, because he will never have any money, although his ransom scheme may be viewed as an attempt to achieve manhood through financial status. She also compromises Bigger when she gets on her knees and prays to Mrs. Dalton not to let her son be executed. But she does love her children, including Bigger, and does the best she can, from her point of view, for them. Bigger's sister and brother are only slightly sketched in as foils to the protagonist: Vera takes sewing lessons at the YWCA, Buddy looks up to his brother.

In contrast to Bigger's family stands that of the Daltons: father, mother, and daughter. Blind Mrs. Dalton (Daltonism is actually the name of a form of color blindness) is from a wealthy family; it is her money that helped her husband launch his lucrative business in real estate. She is well-meaning toward Bigger, encouraging him to return to school, although she has no conception whatsoever that Bigger's problems are far too deep and complicated to be solved by formal education alone. She and her husband donate millions of dollars to the NAACP (the National Association for the Advancement of Colored People), but Bigger has never even heard of it. Mr. Dalton also has no idea of what he is dealing with in Bigger Thomas, as evidenced during his interview with Bigger, when he remarks that he does not think he and his family will have any trouble with Bigger. The owner of the South Side Real Estate Company, which keeps rents high in the city by limiting where blacks can live, Mr. Dalton does not understand at all that he is contributing directly to the making of Bigger Thomases. In fact, he believes himself to be a benefactor of the black community; he is genuinely shocked when Boris Max points out to him that giving Ping-Pong tables to the YMCA is not going to solve the problems of the black community.

The Daltons' daughter, Mary, in contrast to Bigger's girlfriend, Bessie, is a good intentioned but spoiled and ignorant young woman who thinks that black people have so much emotion; she and her boyfriend, Jan, insist that Bigger take them to a black restaurant on his side of town so that they can participate briefly in the "romantic" life of African Americans. They both make Bigger uncomfortable by sitting with him in the front seat of Mr. Dalton's Buick and by forcing him to sit with them in the restaurant. They are oblivious to his presence as they hug and kiss later in the backseat of the car while he drives. To them, Bigger is an unfortunate sociological statistic and potential member of the Communist Party; he is not an individual human being, but instead symbolizes all black people. And yet it is Jan alone (and thus the last name "Erlone") of all the white characters who comes to see Bigger as a human being and not only as a nameless representative of an oppressed minority. Jan is an idealistic young Communist who comes to realize that Bigger's problems led to the killing of his girlfriend; though Jan and Mary really do want to improve conditions for black people, he recognizes the complexity of this issue by the end of the tale.

Bigger's girlfriend, Bessie Mears, leads a miserable life working as a housecleaner for white families; her only relief is alcohol, which Bigger supplies her in exchange for sex. Although she is largely a passive, self-pitying character, this generalization is complicated by the fact that she does point out to Bigger that his killing of Mary Dalton is not made right by the fact that whites have killed far more black people over time. Bigger sees her as a burden that he is not willing to carry; he kills her because he is afraid she will talk to the police. Wright directs our sympathy away from her and toward her killer, even though she is every bit as much a victim as he is, if not more so. But *Native Son* is the story of a black man, not a black woman.

Bigger's lawyer, Boris Max (cf. Marx), has taken on Bigger's case because Buckley has interjected communism as an issue in the trial. Another well-meaning character, he, too, possibly sees Bigger as a member of an exploited class more than as an individual person. At the end of the book, he clearly does not want to accept Bigger's insistent claim that he is what he killed for. The actual person of Bigger is too frightening and complicated for Max's capacities, which are more suited to sociological generalizations, but Max does feel genuine sympathy for his client, and he does try to save his life. The state's attorney, on the other hand, is a cynical manipulator of racial feelings, who sees in the defendant an opportunity to get himself reelected. To Buckley, Bigger is just a guilty and scared young black man from Mississippi (Bigger's family is from that state); it is of no consequence to him that there are extenuating circumstances in the murder of Mary Dalton. He represents the laws that protect the privileges of wealthy whites.

The central character in *Native Son* is indeed a native son, a product of the United States, but not one for whom anyone wants to take responsibility. Three centuries of slavery, oppression, and racism have resulted in the creation of a young black man who is intimidated by whites to such a degree that he accidentally smothers a white woman just so he will not be discovered in her bedroom, which would mean only one thing, rape, as it is a given in his society that a white woman would never voluntarily have sex with a black man. He soon afterward murders a young black woman, his own girlfriend no less, in an extremely brutal manner. He is not, to summarize, a man for whom even bankers' daughters would shed tears, as Wright feared had happened upon the publication of his *Uncle Tom's Children* two years before *Native Son* appeared in 1940.

On one level, then, Bigger is a monster, a killer of two innocent women. Toward the end of his short life, he is alienated from himself, his family, his gang, the black community, the white community—everyone except Jan Erlone and Boris Max, and even they fail to fully understand him. He is a man who takes pleasure in dangling a dead rat in front of his sister's face, in humiliating his friend Gus by making him lick a knife blade, in masturbating in a movie theater (in the 1991 edition), and in demanding ransom money from a dead woman's family. In a word, he seems hopelessly brutalized and stunted.

And yet Wright insists that we ask what caused Bigger to be like this. The answer is suggested in many ways: in his wondering whether he should go to the front or the back of the Daltons' house for his initial job interview; in his intense discomfort at shaking hands with a white man (Jan Erlone) and being told to call him by his first name; in his bitter knowledge that he will never be allowed to pursue his dreams, like learning how to fly a plane; and most frighteningly and dramatically, in his terrified belief that only by smothering Mary Dalton and bludgeoning Bessie Mears can he survive. Every item in the list can be attributed to white racism toward blacks. What Bigger Thomas signifies on this level is that the United States is producing homicidal maniacs in its ghettoes and that its worst nightmares about some young black males are true, but also that American society itself is responsible for its Bigger Thomases.

On another level, though, a more abstract and symbolic level, Bigger Thomas can be interpreted, as he often has been, as a tragic or heroic figure who resists white racism and achieves a measure of understanding and self-determination. The character who is sent to the electric chair at the end of *Native Son* is not just a human version of the rat Bigger killed at the beginning of the narrative. He is someone who has learned a bit about himself and the world he inhabits and he faces the utmost penalty for the crimes he perpetrated in that world, regardless of their source.

The two levels of interpretation do not mesh smoothly, especially when the audience slowly and carefully reads the scenes depicting Bessie Mears's murder or Gus's humiliation. If a reader wants to take Bigger as a metaphor or a symbol for something other than racial hatred and anger, then a great deal of what he does, says, and thinks will have to be downplayed or ignored altogether, which does not seem to be indicative of a judicious reader. And if the character of Bigger Thomas is to be seen as heroic or tragic, then it is hard to see why the same perspective should not be applied to any number of other victims of hostile environments, which trivializes the whole idea of tragedy or heroism. One further difficulty with viewing Bigger in a positive light has to do with the problem of responsibility: if Bigger acted out of uncontrollable fear of whites in the killing of Mary, in what sense is he responsible, and thus a candidate for heroic or tragic stature, for what he did? And as far as environmentalism is concerned, why cannot all the characters Wright holds responsible for the emergence of Bigger, such as Mr. Dalton and Buckley, claim to be products of their environments, too? Interpreting Bigger's character is a fascinating but tricky enterprise. His literary creator may not have had full control of him.

THEMATIC ISSUES

A variety of significant ideas preside over *Native Son*, but they can all be tied to the theme of white racism, which is what produced Bigger Thomas in the first place. To Wright, whites fail to see blacks as human beings; if they did, there would be no Bigger Thomases. But since, as Wright points out, whites think their color is a legitimate source of authority, most are unwilling to relinquish their prejudices because their sense of superiority depends on seeing blackness as a sign of inferiority: acknowledging Bigger's humanity, instead of regarding him as subhuman, would exact a price higher than they are willing to pay—namely, his equality and their concomitant demotion from the top of the racial pyramid. Until whites are willing to admit that their racist attitudes toward people like Bigger and his fellow African Americans are indefensible, Wright's narrative tells us, they can expect to find more and more people like him and perhaps even a racial holocaust that will destroy the entire society—black *and* white. Seen from this perspective, *Native Son* is a warning to the nation that spawned it about the possible outcome of its denial of the humanity of its black citizens.

Reinforcing Wright's attack upon racism is the theme of blindness, in both its literal and metaphorical forms. Mrs. Dalton combines both types of blindness, in that her sightlessness literalizes her inability to see Bigger as just as human as she is. If she could see in the literal sense, the author makes clear, she would see black people only as stereotypes, as figments of her ingrained racist imagination. Mr. Dalton is sighted, but when he looks at Bigger he sees nothing more than an opportunity to reassure himself that he is a friend to the black community by charitably offering employment to an underprivileged youth. When Buckley observes Bigger, he sees only a political opportunity; he does not care what the motivations or reasons may have been for the crimes committed. Boris Max tries hard to understand his client, but his view is so restricted by an exclusive Marxist perspective that he can accept Bigger only as a member of an oppressed social class, not as someone claiming individual value in his acts of violence. Mary Dalton and Jan Erlone see Bigger as a specimen of an exotic and emotional group of people who have been mistreated; after Mary's death, Jan begins to perceive her killer as a fellow human being, but the cost of understanding has been extremely high. And Bigger himself is blind: "He saw Jan as though someone had performed an operation upon his eyes" (333–34). Because Wright equates blindness with lack of understanding, the reader of *Native Son* can see that there is very little understanding in the book; everyone in it, perhaps including the narrator, is blind in one sense or another.

Society's way of seeing—through films, magazines, and newspapers—also contributes to distorted perception. The newspapers in Chicago first report the disappearance of Mary as possibly a Communist plot to divide her father's millions among the poor. Bigger himself is excited by reading about the ransom plot in the newspaper because it seems to validate his actions, but the newspaper also reports as fact that he raped Mary and that he probably had help with the plan of the murder and kidnapping because it was too elaborate for a black mind to conceive. The description of him in the *Tribune* is not a description of a human being, but of a racist caricature: "He [Bigger] is about five feet, nine inches tall and his skin is exceedingly black. His lower jaw protrudes obnoxiously, reminding one of a jungle beast" (322). When Bigger and his buddy Jack go to the movies, they see *Trader Horn*, a popular film of the 1930s that represents Africans as "wild" (37). In the 1940 expurgated version of *Native Son*, Bigger and Jack watch another movie that constructs wealthy whites in a distorted manner, while in the uncensored 1991 version of the novel, Bigger and Jack watch a newsreel about Mary Dalton in which the commentator refers to Mary as a member of the "naughty rich" class (35). Thus, the popular media reflect and cause many of the misperceptions in black and white America.

Bigger's overestimation of Mary Dalton's human worth is connected to his underestimation of the value of the black women in his life: Bessie Mears, Vera Thomas, and Mrs. Thomas. What is really "wrong" with them, from Bigger's point of view, is that they are not white and they are women. He thinks Bessie could be a burden to him in his efforts to escape being caught, but the truth is that he is a far greater burden to her. He regards his sister with such contempt that he has no qualms about causing her to faint by dangling a dead rat in her face. And he resents his mother because she is depicted as valuing him largely in terms of how much money he can bring home, and not as her son. In other words, one of the novel's central concerns is black women; to what extent Wright shares Bigger's anxieties about them is a matter of ongoing debate.

It is important to remember that the setting of *Native Son* also reinforces the environmentalist theme of *Native Son*. Bigger's family left an agrarian way of life for the urban North when it migrated from Mississippi to Chicago, a city to which the Thomases have found hostile and difficult to adjust. It is no accident that Wright chose February as the month the actions in the novel occur because that enables him to use the cold and snow to reinforce the bleakness and hostility of the physical environment: when Bigger flees from the Daltons' house, he leaps out of a window and into a pile of snow that gets into his eyes, mouth, ears, and nose, suggesting that whiteness is overwhelming him. More important than the physical environment, though, is the moral one, for that is what makes Bigger what he is and gives him his values. To what extent Bigger chose his values or they chose him is debatable, but what is clear is that Chicago in the 1930s, the time and place of *Native Son*, is a city of dread, fear, alienation, death, and poverty for black people.

A CINEMATIC READING

One of the more intriguing ways of reading *Native Son*, given the current popularity and influence of interdisciplinary approaches to literature, is to conceive of it in cinematic terms, to consider it for its cinematic qualities and for its connections to films. While two movies based on *Native Son* have been produced, the novel itself can be independently viewed from a cinematic perspective. Informed by numerous references to films in general, as well as by a description of an actual movie, *Trader Horn* (1931), *Native Son* can be seen as a conversation with motion pictures. Its plot is governed by the fact that its "star," Bigger Thomas, is given no role in life, and as a result, he casts himself in his own film, which he also, to a considerable extent, directs. Given Wright's interest in the cinema (he took the role of Bigger Thomas in the first film version of *Native Son*), and further given his fascination with the idea that life itself can be a horror film, it is not surprising that *Native Son* is so cinematic.

The expurgated version of the novel mentions two movies, *Trader Horn* and *The Gay Woman*, the latter of which is fictitious. The unexpurgated version of *Native Son* does not refer to *The Gay Woman*, but it does include references to a newsreel not found in the original 1940 edition of the novel (the newsreel, too, is Wright's invention). Early in the book, Bigger and a member of his gang, Jack Harding, decide to see *Trader Horn*, a real movie first shown in 1931. In contrast to the "Bigger #3" that Wright describes in an essay titled "How Bigger Was Born," who refused to pay for his theater tickets, the Bigger of *Native Son* and his companion buy theirs. Before the newsreel that precedes the feature begins, the two engage in a masturbatory contest that Bigger refers to as "polishing my nightstick" (32). After changing seats so Bigger can better place his feet, the two watch the newsreel about "the daughters of the rich taking sunbaths in the sands of Florida!" (34). To Jack's expressed desire to be in Florida with the daughters of the rich, Bigger replies, "you can. . . . But you'd be hanging from a tree like a bunch of bananas" (34), a statement that reveals Bigger's unconscious acceptance of the notion that African Americans are somehow not fully human, which is also a belief *Trader Horn* will reinforce. The young woman and the young man in the newsreel, whom Bigger sees in close-up, he will soon see in real life in close-up, too, as they are in reality Mary Dalton and Jan Erlone.

Wright is particularly shrewd in his awareness of the film's denial that Africa exists in the present, a denial that a modern audience can see for itself by watching the film on videotape. In the 1930s, when Wright saw the popular film, few African American or non–African American audiences would have been disturbed by its profoundly racist treatment of Africa as frozen in time. As late as the 1920s, for instance, such writers of the Harlem Renaissance as Countee Cullen regarded Africa as an exotic absence (see his poem "Heritage"). When Bigger looks at *Trader Horn*, he sees "pictures of naked men and women whirling in wild dances" (36). Wright's memory is not entirely accurate here, as the Africans are always covered from the waist down (interestingly, the breasts of the African women are uncovered, but the hair of the white "goddess" covers hers). That the film was shot in Kenya, a British colony in the 1930s, adds imperialism to racism. Throughout the film, the Africans are depicted as children who require white direction. The one "good" African is Horn's faithful gun-bearer Ranchero, who responds to every remark Horn sends his way with "*bwana*," a word that has the provocative etymological meaning of "our father." Fortunately for audiences in the 1930s, Ranchero has no sexual interest in the white goddess of the film, as Bigger does in the white goddess of *Native Son*, Mary Dalton.

Horn later exclaims to the character Peru, "That's Africa for you: when you're not eating somebody, you're trying to keep somebody from eating you." Such a remark is exactly what informs the thinking of the racist mobs in *Native Son* that has so terrified Bigger, in part because he represents an Africa that never existed in fact but only in films like *Trader Horn*, in which two white men rescue a white woman who has gone "native" in "deepest, darkest" Africa. As Peru puts it to the white goddess, white people must help one another, an especially ludicrous remark considering who, historically and cinematically speaking, has been a threat to whom.

The narrator of *Native Son* can be challenged in his interpretation of one scene in *Trader Horn*: "He [Bigger] frowned in the darkened movie, hearing the roll of tom-toms and the screams of black men and women dancing free and wild, men and women who were adjusted to their soil and at home in their world, secure from fear and hysteria" (37–38). While the narrator is unquestionably right to resist the power of the film's Eurocentric, allochronic (that is, the idea that a culture exists in some time other than the present, as in some remote past) bias, he may be seeing through Eurocentric eyes himself when he implies that the stereotype the West has of Africa—that it is a highly unified, seamless cultural system—is accurate. There are many different African cultures, all of which are as knowledgeable about fear and hysteria as Bigger is.

Bigger may not be completely aware of the rhetoric of films, but he does know why he sees them. For one thing, they are a source of stimulation in an otherwise empty life. Moreover, to Bigger, movies are an effortless diversion: "He wanted to see a movie; his senses hungered for it. In a movie he could dream without effort; all he had to do was lean back in a seat and keep his eyes open" (13). Movies also provide him with the satisfaction that life denies him: "he was moving toward that sense of fullness that he had so often but inadequately felt in magazines and movies" (170). And yet movies also create desires for fulfillment in Bigger that his actual existence cannot satisfy.

Movies supply Wright's protagonist with more than stimulation, though: they give him partial information about the world and a means of being part of it, at least to some extent. For instance, when Bigger and Gus play at being white, Bigger, pretending to be a general in the army, orders Gus to attack the enemy's left flank. Gus wonders what the left flank is; Bigger answers that he does not know, but he heard about it in the movies. And in the job interview with Mr. Dalton, Bigger knows who Mary is because he saw her in the newsreel. On the other hand, Bigger realizes that although movies refer to the world, they are a distorting window on it; the Mary he sees in real life is very different from the one he saw in the movie theater. The newsreel also enables Bigger to recognize Jan Erlone immediately. And movies give him some modest sense of being a part of the world: "It was when he . . . went to the movies . . . that he felt what he most wanted: to merge himself with others and be a part of this world" (278).

The cinema is everywhere in Wright's novel. The Daltons' previous chauffeur, a man named Green, has pictures of Ginger Rogers, Jean Harlow, and Janet Gaynor (famous stars in the 1930s) on the walls of his room. And once when Bigger dreams, it is about the movie he saw earlier (293). The very language of the book is informed by cinematic figures: "The poster showed one of those faces that looked straight at you . . . and then it stopped, like a movie blackout" (12–13). When Bigger is about to be caught, he observes a man "moving like a figure on the screen in close-up slow motion" (302).

Native Son, then, is shown on a "screen of sober reason" (446), as Boris Max puts it. The director, Richard Wright, intends for his audience to see that this "moving" picture, in two senses of the word, is a metaphor in the process of literalization: if its viewers do not understand the implications of what they are seeing inside Wright's literary theater, then they will see the film again, but outside, in their own homes and on their own streets.

5

Black Boy
(1945, 1991)

Wright was able to carve out such a large piece of the U.S. autobiographical tradition for himself and his life because *Black Boy* is so intensely realized and vivid, especially in Part One. Against irrational but nearly overwhelming power, the hero maintains his integrity and imagination through his determination and persistence. In other words, *Black Boy* is a very American story of a young man's confrontation with a hostile environment, which threatens annihilation if he does not submit to it. But Wright constantly defies the world around him in order to maintain his self-respect and to become the author of *Black Boy*. A system that was designed to crush Wright ironically produced one of its most powerful critics as well as one of the most powerful voices in twentieth-century U.S. literature.

Although the subtitle of Wright's autobiography is "A Record of Childhood and Youth," the book is actually, like any other autobiography, a fictionalized narrative to some degree. *Black Boy* reads more like a novel than a newspaper report because, as his primary biographer, Michel Fabre, has shown, Wright sometimes alters historical facts to suit his thematic concerns. For instance, the narrator relates that the principal of the junior high school from which he graduated as valedictorian tried to interfere with what Wright delivered as a graduation speech, but Fabre points out that the whites were going to allow the principal to start a high school for black students; the principal was understandably upset that Wright might say something that would irritate the whites and thus jeopardize the chance for a black high school, but Wright reports the incident as another attempt to repress him. Or, in a similar vein, Wright claims that he left an optical company where he worked because two white men drove him off; actually, Wright left to return to school in the fall (it may have been Wright's memory that betrayed him here, or it may have been the desire to interpret events to fit the pattern of his autobiography).

It is important to keep another point in mind when reading *Black Boy:* it exists in two editions—the 1945 edition that concludes on an upbeat note as Wright prepares to leave the South for Chicago, and the unexpurgated 1991 edition that includes not only Part Two, which was omitted from the original edition, but also a much more negative ending to Part One. Another revealing difference between the censored 1945 version and the uncensored 1991 version is the crude conversation about Wright's penis by the white optical workers in the 1991 edition, which is cleaned up in the earlier edition. The reader should be cautious, though, about assuming uncritically that censorship always decreases literary quality; it may be the case that the shorter, expurgated version of *Black Boy* is the stronger book, because Part Two lacks the vividness of Part One.

PLOT DEVELOPMENT

In the longer edition, published in 1991, Wright divides the narrative into two parts: Part One—"Southern Night" (Chapters I–XIV); and Part Two—"The Horror and the Glory" (Chapters XV–XX). Both parts turn on the confrontation between the young Richard Wright and a world that is often indifferent at best and murderously hostile at worst. Few life stories begin more sensationally, as the narrator recounts how his four-year-old self set his maternal grandmother's house on fire. Reporting the incident as an accident, Wright unknowingly may be suggesting how resentful and angry he was toward authority and power from the time of his earliest childhood. His family was not the happy black family of the plantation or the minstrel tradition, but a bitterly unhappy one, as least from Wright's perspective. Young Richard was eventually dragged out from underneath the burning house and then lashed so hard that he passed out. Later, he says, "Whenever I tried to sleep I would see huge wobbly white bags, like the full udders of cows, suspended from the ceiling above me" (7). He recalls the event as one in which his mother came close to killing him; he associates death with what should represent love. This single incident, repeated with variations, is the book's entire plot in miniature: self-proclaimed innocence meets with a brutal response at nearly every turn. This opening chapter is also notable for its reference to the first of many moves by the narrator's family, this one from Natchez, Mississippi, to Memphis, Tennessee. All his life, Wright constantly moved around, finally settling in Paris for the last part of his life, but his literary imagination never really left the U.S. South.

One of Wright's earliest encounters with his environment was crucial for him as an eventual writer: unable to sleep one night because of a mewing kitten, Wright's father tells Richard and his brother to kill it, obviously meaning for his words to be taken figuratively. The protagonist sees his chance to resist his father's authority by taking his words literally and so hangs the poor kitten. Language, and how it is taken, can be a weapon, the young Wright realizes, in understanding and controlling the world. But his mother makes him pray over the kitten's grave, which terrifies him and is just one of several episodes in the development of the plot that indicates Wright's condemnation of religion as control of people based upon fear and terror. The opening chapter concludes with Mr. Wright's abandonment of his family for another woman. The narrator goes to considerable effort at the end of this chapter to convince his readers that he did not end up like his father—a poor and ignorant farmer, beaten by life. We also learn that Wright and his brother were eventually placed in an orphanage for a while so that their mother could earn enough to compensate for the loss of Mr. Wright's income.

In Chapter II, Wright leaves the orphanage to move to Elaine, Arkansas, via a trip to Jackson, Mississippi, to visit Granny, Mrs. Wright's mother. There, a schoolteacher named Ella, who is living with Granny, starts to read *Bluebeard and His Seven Wives* to the young Wright; it is a transforming experience, as his starved imagination is fed by the romance and terror of the famous tale. Typically, Granny, with her Seventh-Day Adventist beliefs, dismisses Ella from her house, leaving Wright hungry for more stories of the imagination that could help him make up for the lack of satisfaction that he finds in his encounters with the world. The most vivid incident in the second chapter, though, involves another misreading of the world by the narrator's younger self: Granny is overseeing the bathing of her two grandsons, when she tells the older one to bend over so she can scrub his anus; Wright tells her to kiss back there when she is finished washing. Granny is so offended by Wright's impertinence that she starts beating him with a wet towel. Once again, the author is dramatizing through plot development that his naive young self was traumatized in its engagements with the environment, but the episode is also another lesson in the extreme power of words: language is like the food of life to Wright, and he could never get enough. Chapter II also includes the killing of Wright's Uncle Hoskins, who was murdered by whites who coveted his lucrative saloon business; this racial violence taught Wright what the ultimate consequence of his encounters with the whites could be.

The next chapter centers on the narrator's relationship with his mother after she suffers a paralytic stroke. Granny comes to help, but Wright's mother suffers another stroke. One night she calls her oldest son to her bed to tell him her pain is so bad that she wants to die. The narrator tells us that that "night I ceased to react to my mother; my feelings were frozen" (117). At the age of 12, the narrator was convinced "that the meaning of living came only when one was struggling to wring a meaning out of meaningless suffering"(118). His craving for maternal affection was never satisfied; and, in fact, the plot of *Black Boy* supports the notion that Wright's hunger for love in general was never satisfied when he was young.

The plot of Chapter IV is driven by Wright's condemnation of religion as an institution that bases truth on authority rather than on evidence, or, to put it another way, as an institution that does not distinguish between truth and belief, a distinction Wright thought crucial. To his maternal grandmother, Seventh-Day Adventism (a religion that treats Saturday as the seventh day of the week and believes that Christ's second coming to earth and the Last Judgment are imminent) was absolutely true and beyond challenge. As a rationalist, a skeptic, and a one-worlder (someone who believes that there is at most one world and that we are in it), Wright could not help but disagree with Granny in the strongest way, but he sympathizes with and understands her hunger for what he believes reality does not offer: miracles, eternal life, the supernatural. In an attempt to placate her, he tells her that if he ever sees an angel, he will regard it as proof that she is right—in actuality, if Wright ever had such an experience, he would have consulted a doctor—but Granny mishears him, thinking he said that he did see an angel, which temporarily makes her deeply pleased with her grandson. When she learns the truth, she is more disappointed than ever with him. But Wright's point is that in his encounters with the world, he refuses to sacrifice his integrity to suit either people or convenience. As this incident in the plot, along with many others, proves, *Black Boy* is very much about the growth of a young writer in a world that wanted to destroy his ambition to write and to think for himself. It is this desire to control Wright's thinking that governs his Aunt Addie to compromise her nephew before his classmates when she demands that he reveal who is dropping walnut shells on the floor of her classroom; according to the young Wright's code, one does not tell on a peer (Wright was not the culprit), but Aunt Addie is so angry that she cannot bend him to her will that Wright, in self-defense, pulls a knife on her when they are at Granny's house after school. The plot supports Wright's contention that if he had not had such a strong will, he would never have written *Black Boy.*

The rest of the plot of Part One is shaped largely by three key developments: the humiliating treatment by a white woman who scoffs at the narrator's literary ambitions, the narrator's determination to leave the South, and his hunger for reading. The condescending white woman at the beginning of Chapter VI is considering Wright for domestic work at her house when she asks him if he steals: whether this incident actually occurred or not, it does make Wright's undebatable point that he and his fellow blacks were regarded as a species of children by whites, the latter of whom refused to believe they could not legitimately ask such questions of black people. Worse, though, is her attitude toward the narrator's desire to become a writer: the very idea of a black boy wanting to write is one she automatically and indignantly rejects. It is this appalling arrogance—whites' sureness that they know what the proper place in the world for blacks is—that Wright finds so offensive. Soon after this incident, Wright did produce a story titled "The Voodoo of Hell's Half-Acre," and published it in a black newspaper, although no copy of the story has been found.

The plot of Part One moves all along toward the narrator's decision to leave the South, because his temperament is inimical to a world based on the lie that whites are superior to blacks. Why, the narrator asks himself, should he remain in an environment where his primary racial function seems to be to reassure whites who they are? Since it is a lack of money that prevents him from leaving this world, the young Wright sets about trying to accumulate funds as expeditiously as possible. To finance his trip northward, he gets involved in schemes to steal movie tickets, a gun, and cans of fruit preserves. Arriving in Memphis in November 1925, he stays with a Mrs. Moss and her daughter, Bess, who try to control him by getting him to marry Bess (Fabre has pointed out that Wright was not as sexually restrained with Bess as he claims he was).

By the end of Part One, the narrator has become a voracious reader, devouring books and magazines at every opportunity in order to satisfy an intellectual appetite that had been denied nourishment. He begins reading *Harper's Magazine*, *Atlantic Monthly*, and *American Mercury*, and he uses a note with a forged white man's signature on it in order to check out books from a library in Memphis by H. L. Mencken, an aggressive social critic of the 1920s. Reading was Wright's salvation, for it took him to intellectual places the white South had forbidden him to enter. It also made him see that the written word could be a weapon he could use against a world that wanted to control him. Books helped give Wright what his environment did not. As the narrator says, "All my life had shaped me for the realism, the naturalism of the modern novel, and I could not read enough of them" (295).

The 1945 edition of *Black Boy* ends at the point of the narrator's departure for the North, and on a relatively optimistic note, perhaps caused by pressure to be hopeful because the United States was fighting World War II in 1945. But the notion that the 1991 conclusion of Part One, more negative in tone, is superior, is challengeable. It does not necessarily follow that censorship always results in inferior writing. The expurgated ending, for example, contains a key passage in which Wright relates how the white South told him who he was—namely, a "nigger"—but Wright points out that the white South had never known him, so it could not have known what he was. At the very least, contemporary readers of *Black Boy* should compare both endings to Part One for themselves.

Wright organizes the plot of Part Two, "The Horror and the Glory" (the horror and the glory of communism, that is), around several key episodes: his employment by a couple named the Hoffmans, the "Finnish cook incident," his work at a medical research institute, his experience with the John Reed Club, and his falling out with the Communist

Party. Soon after Wright arrives in Chicago in 1927, he begins working as a porter for the Hoffmans, owners of a grocery. Because of his Southern background, he misunderstands their spoken English. Told to get a can of chicken à la king at a neighboring store, for example, Wright asks for a can of "Cheek Keeng Awr Lar Keeng" (311). More serious is his lying to the Hoffmans about why he missed work one day: he tells them his mother has died, when in fact he was simply out applying for a better job. This disappoints the Hoffmans, who are not concerned about Richard being black, but they do not appreciate fully his fear of giving offense to a white employer.

Soon afterward, he takes a job as a dishwasher at a restaurant, where the cook is an elderly Finnish woman. To Wright's horror, he sees the cook spit in the boiling soup. In a sane society, of course, Wright would have told the owner of the restaurant immediately, but in the United States of the 1920s, he knows the word of a black man might be questioned, especially since, if whites are superior, no one in their racial category would spit in the soup. So he tells a black woman who makes salads in the restaurant about the cook. The owner reluctantly listens to her because the owner does not assume automatically that she is a liar.

His work as an orderly in a medical research institute in Chicago includes the horrible but absurd description of medical experiments; two other orderlies, Brand and Cooke, get into a childish argument that turns into life-threatening violence as they lunge at each other with an ice pick and a knife. The fighting knocks the animal cages about so much that the rabbits and guinea pigs escape from their cages. To keep their jobs, the orderlies put them back into their cages in a helter-skelter manner, which almost certainly skewed the results of the medical experiments that were being performed on them. But in the United States, Wright contends, he and his fellow blacks "had made . . . [their] own code of ethics, values, loyalty" (370).

Key developments in Wright's literary career are set in motion when he is invited to join the John Reed Club, named after the only U.S. citizen buried at the base of the wall around the Kremlin in Moscow. The series of clubs bearing his name provided radical young writers like Wright with a supportive audience and the opportunity to publish in leftist literary magazines: as the narrator puts it, "here at last in the realm of revolutionary expression was where Negro experience could find a home, a functioning value and role" (375).

Wright is also attracted to communism at this time because black equality is one of its major tenets. Early on in his career as a Communist, though, he develops misgivings: a fellow Communist disapproves of a book he is reading as bourgeois, and Wright is told that intellectuals such as himself do not fit well into the Communist Party, which he had joined in order to continue as secretary of his branch of the John Reed Club. Furthermore, he is instructed to write political pamphlets. In other words, the Communist Party began to suggest lack of free speech and expression to Wright; so in a sense, he feels he is right back in the South again. The writers and artists in the clubs are concerned with artistic growth, while the Party is more concerned with its political development. Although the clubs and Communism were both a large part of Wright's life, the clubs mattered more.

Eventually, the whole chain of John Reed Clubs is dissolved at a writers conference Wright attends in New York City, which leaves him free of all party ties. His relationship with communism hits a new low when two white Communists assault him on May Day in 1936 because he was considered a traitor. The plot of the 1991 version of *Black Boy* ends with the narrator pledging to himself to "create a sense of the hunger for life that gnaws in us all" (453).

CHARACTER DEVELOPMENT

Character development in *Black Boy* is closely connected to its presiding theme: the clash between the sensitive and imaginative hero, Richard Wright, and his antagonistic environment. Besides Wright himself, the central characters include his parents and his maternal grandmother. Writing about his mother is very painful for Wright, because she had to endure so much undeserved and pointless suffering and because he felt he never received sufficient emotional support from her. He also never understood her nearly beating him to death for setting his grandmother's house on fire in the introductory chapter of *Black Boy*. His mother's character, in other words, is very much a part of the oppressive environment in which the narrator grew up, but she herself is also very much a victim of it. Abandoned by her husband, Mrs. Wright is left with the responsibility of rearing her two sons at a time when black women could make very little money and had very few options. Complicating her plight are several paralytic strokes that leave her bedridden for long stretches of time. In the narrator's imagination, she comes to be emblematic of the pointlessness of so much human suffering. On the other hand, Mrs. Wright encouraged Richard to learn how to read, and her son knows she loves him, even if not enough from his perspective.

The narrator views his father, too, as a victim of an environment far stronger than he was. Mr. Wright walked out on his wife and two sons for another woman, but he ended up a broken man, "a sharecropper, clad in ragged overalls" (40), as the narrator describes him in highly socially inflected language at the conclusion of Chapter I. I am not my father's son, is Wright's implicit position whenever he remembers his father. He particularly recalls him as a glutton around a little boy who was perpetually hungry: "He was quite fat and his bloated stomach lapped over his belt" (11). The narrator's lasting attitude toward his father, though, is relief—relief that he did not turn out the way his father did, a man viewed by his son as totally defeated by the world around him.

Along with the narrator himself, the strongest-willed character in *Black Boy* is Granny, Mrs. Wright's mother and a woman who could have passed for white. Her response to the physical world in which she lives is to reject it in favor of another eternal one elsewhere, however misguided this seems to her grandson. She embraces Seventh-Day Adventism without reservation and tries to make her grandson do the same; the result is an inevitable confrontation, because she and the narrator are both very strong-minded people. Her determination to make Wright a Seventh-Day Adventist makes sense, given her certainty that her religious views are unchallengeable. It is clear, though, that in her own way, she loves the narrator, because when he asserts that he will leave her house if he is not allowed to work on Saturdays, the day of worship for Seventh-Day Adventists, she relents, which is a major concession to human feelings on the part of such an uncompromising person. Granny and the narrator are more alike than either realizes. On the other hand, she is extremely narrow-minded, throwing a boarder out of her house merely for reading *Bluebeard and His Seven Wives* to her grandson and using her religion as a means of attempted control over him. Nor does she make any effort to avoid striking the narrator frequently and sometimes arbitrarily.

But in his role of dominant character in *Black Boy*, Wright triumphs over an ugly world, for it is he who grew up to write the book. There is distance between Wright the narrator in *Black Boy* and Wright the character. For one thing, the narrator is looking back, through time and memory, at his younger self. The narrator is particularly anxious that his readers not conclude that he writes the way his character sometimes spoke then; in other words, Wright as narrator and writer does not want us to think he is a victim of his linguistic environment or that he would ever have written the black English he sometimes spoke. The narrator also wants to make it clear beyond any doubt that the character Wright did not grow up to be another version of his father, that the social environment did not destroy him the same way it destroyed his father.

The hero of *Black Boy*, Richard Wright the character, has an extremely strong personality, a necessity if he wants to struggle successfully against his environment. Without a generous supply of determination and will, he would have become what the system around him was designed to force him to become: a subhuman creature. When the white woman who asks him if he steals laughs at his literary ambitions, it hurts his feelings, but this incident leaves him all the more determined to succeed as a writer. When Granny and his mother force him to be "saved," he conforms outwardly but maintains his inner integrity, thereby implying what he thinks about institutionalized religion.

Yet there is a softer side to Wright's personality as it encounters the surrounding world, a very lyrical and imaginative side that reveals itself perhaps most strikingly in its reactions to nature. Early in *Black Boy*, Wright notes "the yearning for identification loosed in . . . [him] by the sight of a solitary ant carrying a burden upon a mysterious journey" (8) and "the incomprehensible secret embodied in a whitish toadstool hiding in the dark shade of a rotting log" (9). To compensate for the perceived bleakness of the outer world, Wright cultivated a rich inner world where his sensibility could have free reign. It is this facet of his character that almost always finds the social environment a severe disappointment.

His most salient trait, though, is his hunger for life itself. It is when the world prevents him from satisfying the craving that he is most unhappy. More than most people, Wright could not bear missing out on life's opportunities; and, of course, he did miss out on many of them. But his resourcefulness, toughness, and intelligence enabled him to write one of the most remarkable autobiographies in U.S. literature. The irony in the development of his character is that if the world had provided him with more nourishment, he might well not have become the powerful writer he is regarded as now. This is not to say that what he went through is to be recommended or that it usually produces great writers, but only to note the irony. He could never read or write enough books, have enough experiences, visit enough places. He was hyper-aware of what he was missing. Basically, what Wright wanted to do was devour the world around him.

Wright's desire to consume, however, should be juxtaposed with his honesty and trustworthiness. Growing up in a world that said black boys were liars, Wright the character tries to tell the truth, although sometimes Wright the narrator's memory may have betrayed him or his imagination may have seduced him. It is difficult, though, to be the reporter of one's own honesty, and so some readers of *Black Boy* have wondered if Richard Wright was really the only sensitive young black person in his community, or if he really did not understand the meaning of his words when he told Granny "to kiss back there," or if he was always the innocent victim of a hostile environment.

THEMATIC ISSUES

Black Boy is informed by numerous themes, but perhaps the overriding one is the hero's engagement with his environment. It is Wright against the world in *Black Boy*, with the world unremittingly cruel and much more powerful but with Wright never surrendering, never letting the world around him gain a complete and final victory. Readers cannot help but admire how undaunted the hero usually is, no matter how many times he gets knocked down. What enabled this extreme resiliency was his toughness and strong-mindedness. Wright can serve as a model for anyone struggling against a system that denies a person's humanity. Like Malcolm X and Frederick Douglass, the hero of *Black Boy* ultimately becomes famous and successful.

Closely allied to the book's presiding theme is that of hunger, as is suggested by the original title for the unexpurgated version, *American Hunger*. Wright went hungry in the literal sense many times when he was growing up. Sometimes he would wake up at night to find hunger standing at his bedside, and at the orphanage where his mother placed him for a time, he was often too weak from hunger to help with pulling the grass that had to be pulled by hand. The notion of hunger also inflects the language of *Black Boy*: "I had tasted what to me was life" (47), the narrator remarks after hearing *Bluebeard and His Seven Wives* read aloud to him. Later, he mentions that he was "starved" (178) for contact with other people and that he "hungered for books" (294). He was starving for understanding, love and approval, formal education, opportunity, freedom, ideas, recognition, money, and fulfillment, but in the South and the North of the United States in the first third of the twentieth century, practically no black person's appetite for such sustenance could be satisfied.

For a potential writer, of course, a craving for language and literacy is a necessary appetite. Wright learned to make sense out of "the baffling black print" (25) at a young age. And when he heard the story of Bluebeard, "reality changed, the look of things altered, and the world became peopled with magical presences" (45). His forged library card is in the tradition of slaves who forged their own passes to leave plantations. Wright understood, like Malcolm X did when he memorized an English dictionary in prison, that language in its spoken and printed forms, would give him a measure of control and freedom in a world designed to deny him both. Writing, for Wright, was the equivalent of Seventh-Day Adventism for his maternal grandmother. Without it, he might have become some variant of Bigger Thomas.

In particular, writing helped Wright explore the issue of race, another significant idea in *Black Boy*. That racism is an effect of ignorance on the part of whites is one of the points the book drives home over and over. If Wright is subhuman, how does he manage to produce such a remarkable autobiography? If whites are "superior," why is Wright smarter than they are? It is clear in *Black Boy* that the idea of racial inequality has been perpetuated by whites to justify their privileges and advantages over blacks, but it has no legitimate basis otherwise. And although their advantages are based on a self-created division among otherwise equal persons, whites are not willing to forgo their advantages voluntarily. Wright makes this racial point humorously when he records that as a child, he would follow a crowd of black children to a row of privies, where the black kids would watch people of all colors release excretions of the same color. And yet what is absurd, ridiculous, and irrational—racial privilege—gets black people killed and humiliated. *Black Boy* protests this notion loudly and eloquently in an effort to stop it, but as Wright knew all too well, racism is one of humanity's most pernicious beliefs, one that may never be completely exterminated. Nevertheless, Wright makes an irrefutable case in his autobiography that a person's humanity must be accepted on faith;

any test of it or definition of it automatically excludes some people from the category.

Two other significant ideas that are developed in *Black Boy* are violence and religion, both as a means of control. Each of these themes is connected directly to the book's overarching concern with Wright versus the world. The violence is everywhere in *Black Boy*, a narrative that begins with the hero being beaten into unconsciousness for setting his grandparents' house on fire and ends with him being assaulted by two Communists in 1936. In between, he is hit and slapped repeatedly, mainly by members of his own family. Once, he is strongly criticized for dodging a blow from Granny, which results in her losing her balance and hurting herself. On another occasion, Wright reports that he and another young black man named Harrison end up fighting each other to amuse older white men. Wright himself threatens one of his uncles with razor blades (the uncle was going to whip him) and pulls a knife on his Aunt Addie (he was terrified at what she might do to him). Wright continually faces a world that relies on force, rather than sound judgment and truth, to get its way, a world that readily substitutes emotion for thought. As such, *Black Boy* is a plea for rationality over physicality. If the world is right, the narrator frequently wonders, why does it rely on force instead of argument? The answer is that the world is not right; instead, it is mindless and violent. The world does not explain; it attacks. Rather than just accept this, Wright resists it through reason and imagination.

The world of *Black Boy* also has another means of control in its arsenal: religion. What religion is after, in Wright's view, is social conformity; in other words, religion is just another worldly institution, like his family, that wants him to fit in, to accept without questioning, and it is not subtle about how it brings about this conformity. In the case of his mother's Methodism, Wright and some other young black men in the book act like they are believers, because if they do not, their refusal will be taken as evidence that they do not love their mothers. Religion is thus a cover for power that is based, not on reason, but on the self-aggrandizement of its adherents.

Wright confronted religion from the perspective of someone who believes in one world against religion's claim that there is another one, a claim Wright found redundant. That is to say, where is this other world? How does one get to it? Why would one want to go there, considering who else might be there? Wright does not consider religion intellectually respectable because it talks about an unseen world in terms of this seen one, which does not make sense to him. The narrator believes that there is at most one world and that we are in it, so the only thing we can talk about sensibly is that realm we physically inhabit. What Wright may not have given enough thought to in his criticism of religion, though, is that the black church traditionally has been, at least until recently, the center of the black community and the only institution in the United States that African Americans have controlled. He also may not have given enough attention to the theory that heaven and hell, for instance, even if incoherent notions, may be the necessary "sizzle" to bring people to religion and keep them there; religion may need imaginary carrots and sticks to encourage such secular virtues as kindness and charity.

A CULTURAL READING

A particularly effective way of unlocking the assumptions implicit in *Black Boy* is through the lens of cultural critique, a way of reading a text that challenges what writers and their audiences often take for granted as "natural" rather than human constructions. For instance, in *Beloved*, Toni Morrison assumes that it goes without saying that a black man cannot be heroic and gay, which suggests her uncritical acceptance of a cultural norm over something that is actually the case. Or, to take another example, the nineteenth-century British novelist Thomas Hardy, in *Tess of the D'Urbervilles*, never questions the assumption that happiness for his heroine lies in a heterosexual relationship within the institution of marriage. Similarly, Wright accepts in his autobiography a set of axioms about social class, race, and gender that can be profitably examined, as opposed to merely accepted or ignored altogether. In making assumptions, or in being the product of them, Wright is doing what we all inevitably do when trying to make sense of the world. But cultural critique can make us aware of our assumptions, which in turn can then be subjected to analytical scrutiny.

Unrecognized assumptions about social class are everywhere in *Black Boy*. For example, although Wright despised the black middle class, he was evidently no fan of the black lower class either, for he was deeply concerned that his readers not think he could end up like his father, a "black peasant." He seems to believe that this would be a horrific fate, one to be avoided at any cost, a kind of social hell. A dubious social perspective also informs Wright's reactions to the black families he sees when he works as an assistant to an insurance agent named Brother Nance: "Many of the naive black families bought their insurance from us because they felt that they were connecting themselves with something that would make their children 'write'n speak lak dat pretty boy from Jackson' " (160). He later refers to such people as "walleyed yokels" (161), an unfortunate phrase that suggests Wright's social prejudices. He is intellectually aware that social classes are not natural entities because at one point in *Black Boy* he uses the phrase "the artificial status of race and class" (218), but this intellectual awareness about artificial social distinctions does not regulate his feelings about social class.

Race- and gender-based assumptions can also be discovered throughout *Black Boy*. At the end of Chapter I, for instance, the narrator observes that his father had not been handed a chance to learn about loyalty, sentiment, and tradition by the white landowners. The reader might well ask why Wright's father could not have learned about these values from the black community, which was just as knowledgeable about them as the white community; however, Wright may sometimes see his own community through white eyes. The most notorious example of Wright's uncritical deployment of race-based assumptions is the passage early in Chapter II, where the narrator mulls "over the strange absence of real kindness in Negroes" and contends that black people "had never been allowed to catch the full spirit of Western civilization" (43). African Americans are as kind as anybody else, and they have developed their own cultural traditions out of the intersection of African and European cultures, but Wright may have so internalized the perspective of the majority culture that he cannot see its own limitations, anymore than people now can see without blind spots. The same Richard Wright who can acknowledge the "artificial status of race and class" (218) in the middle of *Black Boy*, and so is not completely in the grip of the notion of white as the norm, only a little later refers to "a pale yellow" African American who has gonorrhea and was proud of that fact, a reference that may betray intraracial racism in the narrator. In a society as race-bound as the United States, though, it may be asking too much of anyone to see through all its racial deceptions. Also, one should give Wright some credit for his honesty about the issue of race: not everyone, for example, would write, "I felt—but only temporarily—that perhaps the whites were right, that

Negroes were children and would never grow up" (431). This remark comes out of his temporary frustration with black actors who appear in a play the public might not like. The reader should also consider that everyone, including him or herself is inevitably a product of a particular time and place. This fact does not justify Wright's attitude toward the actors but may help to explain it.

In addition to assumptions governing Wright's attitudes toward race and social class, there are gender-based suppositions that can be detected throughout *Black Boy*. It seems odd, for instance, for Wright to refer to his adult Aunt Jody as a "girl" (104), and it is embarrassing to read that Granny and Aunt Addie became so hostile toward him that they ordered him to wash and iron his own clothes, as if such work were the ultimate debasement. In one church he attended, he notes the presence of "wobbly-bosomed black and yellow church matrons" and "skinny old maids" (178), women he looks *at* but not *with*. More troubling, perhaps, is an incident involving a young black woman Wright observes as a white policeman slaps her on the buttocks; when Wright asks her how she can stand that kind of treatment, she replies that it does not matter. In response to her comment that he would have been a fool if he had done something about it, he tells her he would have been, meaning he would have been a fool to try to do something for her. She misses the point, according to the narrator, but we may wonder if Wright does not miss the point when he gives no consideration to why she might tolerate disrespectful treatment from a white man: doing anything else could have resulted in horrible consequences to her and to Wright. His attitude toward the white waitresses he works with in Chicago may also reveal a failure of empathy and imagination on his part: the reader should question why it is necessarily so bad that the "words of their souls were the syllables of popular songs" (321). Equally disturbing is his reference to a woman he dislikes for regarding him as an Uncle Tom: "a huge, fat, black woman" (432).

The worst combination for Wright is a poor, black woman because that combination embodies his deepest anxieties about social class, race, and gender (but we should keep in mind that Bessie Mears, in *Native Son*, while an example of this category, nevertheless points out to Bigger Thomas that the fact that whites have killed many blacks, does not justify his killing Mary Dalton). In *Black Boy*, the young black woman with whom Wright has sex in exchange for his paying her insurance premiums (340–43) is probably the best example of this phenomenon: not only is she poor, black, and a woman, but she is also an illiterate obsessed with the notion of seeing a circus. Wright finds her beyond his understanding because she differs so much from him that he cannot identify with her. But then, why sleep with what is perplexing and without value? And what does such a relationship suggest about Wright?

Like anybody else, Wright reflects many of the unexamined assumptions of a particular time and place: his attitudes toward black women in his autobiography are far from unique; this is not to justify but to explain them. And it is also pertinent to consider that because one is oneself a victim of prejudice, it hardly follows that one will be any less a victimizer than anyone else. Nor does a cultural reading of *Black Boy* support a sense of moral and/or intellectual superiority on the part of the reader, but it does open up the book in revealing ways that can deepen our understanding of it, and of the author and times that produced it.

The Outsider
(1953)

The Outsider is an ambitious novel, the first novel Wright published since *Native Son* came out in 1940. It is a long, complex investigation into, among other issues, the limits of human freedom. Wright is interested here in finding out how far one man, Cross Damon, can go and still be counted as part of society. The answer seems to be, not as far as he had thought, for Wright's protagonist pays dearly for violating the social conventions that regulate human behavior, although he had assumed that there would be no real consequences to his contempt for the restraint that governs most people's lives much of the time.

PLOT DEVELOPMENT

Consisting of five books, the highly episodic plot of *The Outsider* is used as a trellis to support the novel's philosophical speeches. Book One, "Dread," opens with an epigraph from the Danish philosopher of dread, Søren Kierkegaard: "Dread is an alien power which lays hold of an individual and yet one cannot tear oneself away, nor has a will to do so; for one fears what one desires" (369). Like *Lawd Today!* and *Native Son, The Outsider* begins in Chicago during the wintertime. We view four black post office workers after work on their way to the Salty Dog to have a drink. Of the four—Booker, Cross Damon (the outsider), Joe Thomas, and Pink—one, Cross, suffers from the four A's: alcohol, abortion, automobiles, and alimony. As they walk, the men laugh about how Cross used to throw silver coins out of the eleventh-floor window of the post office to watch the antlike people below scramble to collect them, which made Cross feel like God, a prospective irony in light of the fact that he will soon act like he is God.

Cross has a child, a teenager named Dot, for a mistress, and the affair has caused him to be estranged from his wife, Gladys. His personal problems have led him to consider suicide. Cross and his wife have three children, and Dot is pregnant by Cross. We also learn that Cross is 26 years old and was born in 1924, which makes the novel set in 1950. Cross's plan is to unload Dot, but when he arrives at her apartment early in the book, a doctor and Dot's girlfriend Myrtle are there. Another friend of Dot's named May calls Dot while he is there, but Cross takes the call only to discover that May has found a lawyer to "tie up Damon" (407): since Dot is under 16, a legal minor, Cross can be found guilty of statutory rape if she presses charges against him. In the very emotional confrontation between the two lovers, Cross makes clear that he wants Dot to abort the child, but she refuses; she also tells him that hiring the lawyer was Mary's idea and that she lied about her age to him because she liked him.

Wright then provides us with background information about Gladys. Like her husband, Gladys is an outsider, having attended an integrated school where she never felt accepted. She also hates white people because they are different from her. While Gladys was in the hospital giving birth to their son Cross Jr., Cross went on a drinking binge with Pink, Joe, and Booker. Returning home with baby Cross and a nurse, Gladys found her husband in bed with a girl. Back in the fictional present, Cross realizes that he does not love his wife and may never have loved her. In his determination to find a way to make her hate him, he goes home from the post office one morning and gratuitously slaps her; he slaps her again in an apparent effort to cause her to think he is unbalanced. He pretends to remember nothing about the incident when he returns from the Salty Dog, but on an Easter Sunday morning, he repeats his first attack. When he again returns from the bar, Gladys points his gun at him, demanding that he get out.

The plot then makes a crucial and dramatic shift: on the way to see Dot, Cross is caught in a subway accident; because his overcoat is found near a victim of the accident who shares Cross's build, it is assumed that the dead man is Cross. The real Cross Damon decides to let the world, including his three sons, think that he was killed in the subway accident. He now has an opportunity to put into play the "fondest and deepest conviction of his life," namely, "[t]hat all men were free" (457). Renaming himself Charles Webb from Memphis, Cross resolves to go to New York to begin his new adventure as a self-constructed man: "The question summed itself up: What's a man? He had unknowingly set himself a project of no less magnitude than contained in that awful question" (460–61). Before leaving, though, he tells a prostitute in a hotel about the subway accident (nothing comes of this revelation), then he encounters Joe and hits him in the temple with an empty whiskey bottle before throwing him out a window. This is the first of many murders committed by the protagonist. Joe has to be killed if the world is to believe that Cross died in the subway accident.

Book Two, "Dream," begins with a paranoid Cross on a train to New York. In his car, he encounters several more characters: a priest, Father Seldon; the priest's friend, Ely Houston, who is a "celebrated crime-buster" (497) and the district attorney of New York City (and, as a hunchback, also an outsider); and Bob Hunter, a black waiter on the train, who asks Cross to testify that it was a white woman's fault that a pot of coffee fell on her. Cross is now identifying himself as one Addison Jordan. After he and Houston discuss how black people are outsiders, Cross remarks to Houston, "Maybe man is nothing in particular" (507), which is probably the sentence in *The Outsider* that is most frequently quoted by commentators.

Arriving in Harlem, Cross rents a room from a Hattie Turner. He then goes to a cemetery, where he finds the name and life span of his next assumed identity, Lionel Lane. To obtain Lane's birth certificate, Cross pretends to be an idiot in front of the clerks responsible for releasing such data. Later on, he visits Bob Hunter and his wife Sarah, the former of whom is the waiter from the train, who has now lost his job because of the confrontation with the white woman on the train. Cross learns that Bob, from Trinidad, works for the Communist Party, which Cross soon joins, too, not because he desires to, but because he sees a purpose in joining: since Communists are also outsiders, they can serve as camouflage from the law. Cross hopes, as well, that membership among them could ease his loneliness and isolation.

Gil and Eva Blount then arrive at Bob's apartment: Gil is a member of the Central Committee of the Communist Party; and, as we learn later, Eva is his deeply unhappy wife, who was tricked into marrying him. Gil promises to pay for Cross to go the Workers' School if he will agree to live with Gil and Eva for political purposes. Then, Jack Hilton, another Communist Party official, comes to Bob's apartment and orders Bob to stop organizing Communist cells in the Dining Car Waiters' Union. When Bob protests that he intends to continue his organizing activities, Hilton threatens that the party will kill him. All this activity seems to stimulate Cross: "Cross felt that he was at last awaking. The dream in which he had lived since he fled Chicago was leaving him. The reality about him was beginning to vibrate: he was slowly becoming himself again, but it was a different self" (571).

The third book of *The Outsider*, "Descent," follows the movement of Cross into the depths of the Communist Party. Gil wants to stop his landlord, Langley Herndon, from discriminating against blacks, which is why he invited Cross to move in with him and Eva. While she is out one day, Cross examines a painting of Eva's for two hours and also reads her diary; from it, he learns why Eva is so miserable: Gil was ordered by the party to marry her. In one entry, she writes that she met an American expatriate in Paris who told her that Rose Lampkin, Gil's secretary, is not only her husband's mistress, but that she is spying on him as well. This knowledge causes Eva to walk the streets of Paris for a day to keep thoughts of suicide from filling her head. She even sleeps with a knife under her pillow thereafter in case Gil tries to touch her. Eva therefore sympathizes with black people because of the way she has been treated; she understand their alienation and their sense of having only a peripheral status.

After the episode of reading Eva's diary, Cross himself encounters the racist landlord Langley Herndon, who orders him out of the building and even threatens to kill him. Then Bob Hunter comes to Gil's apartment to see Gil; he wants Gil to help him get back into the party, which has since expelled him. In the meantime, Cross hears voices in Herndon's apartment, where he discovers Gil and Herndon fighting each other. Eva soon follows Cross to the horrible scene of Herndon beating Gil with a fire poker. Eva runs away, at which point Cross proceeds to kill both men in a manner that makes it look like the two men killed each other.

"Despair," the penultimate book of *The Outsider*, begins with Cross's phone call to Hilton to inform him about the deaths of Herndon and Blount; consequently, accompanied by a man named Menti, Hilton appears at Eva's apartment (he seems to suspect Cross in the recent killings). Cross considers that "he was staring right now at the focal point of modern history: if you fought men who tried to conquer you in terms of total power you had to use total power and in the end you became what you tried to defeat" (632). Hilton remarks to Cross that he always hated Gil, whose real name was Bernstein, and he tells Eva to pretend that she does not know Gil is dead: she is to start screaming when she "learns" he is dead. When the police arrive, Hilton accuses them of racism toward "Lionel Lane." Ely Houston, the district attorney Cross met on the train to New York, will investigate the double murder. To get rid of the handkerchief Cross bloodied when he killed Blount and Herndon before Houston is expected to appear the next morning, Cross puts it in the incinerator. Hilton sees him do this, but Cross covers by saying that he was simply disposing of a cigarette.

The following morning, accompanied by a medical examiner, Dr. Stockon, Houston indeed appears at Gil's apartment. The examiner explains to Houston that although it is strange that both victims were seemingly hit by the fire poker and a table leg, it is possible. When Dr. Stockton further says that it is possible that a third party killed both victims, Houston seems to scoff at the idea. Houston tells Cross that if a third person killed both the victims, that person would have had to believe "[t]hat no ideas are necessary to justify his acts" (671), a remark that causes Cross to realize that Houston is on the right track. Houston then reveals that he knows all three men—Gil, Hendon, and the imaginary third person—are psychologically similar because he himself identifies with them: Houston regards ideas like communism and fascism as after-the-fact justifications for feelings. Finally in the scene, Eva tells Cross that if he leaves, she will kill herself. What she does not yet know about this man to whom she apparently feels connected is that Cross is precisely what she hates: someone who uses other people and organizations solely for his own benefit.

Sarah then comes to Eva's apartment to inform Cross and Eva that immigration has arrested Bob, a clear indication that the party betrayed him. It is this revelation that leads Cross to consider killing Hilton, whom he blames for Bob's problems with the party. Arriving at Hilton's hotel, Cross is told that he is not in his room, so he wanders the streets, asking himself, "[w]as it that he had gotten himself into such an emotional state that nothing meant anything anymore, or was it that *too* much meaning had now entered his life, more meaning than he could handle?" (683). Cross returns to Hilton's hotel and is able to enter his room this time, as the maid has left the door open temporarily. In Hilton's room, Cross discovers not only the bloody handkerchief he thought he dropped in the incinerator, but also a .32 caliber pistol, which he proceeds to unload. Upon Hilton's return to his room, Cross reveals that he has found the bloody handkerchief. Hilton admits that he is glad Cross killed Gil because Gil had a job in the party that Hilton wanted and also because Hilton is romantically interested in Eva. He tells Cross to sweep "your illusions aside. . . . Get down to what is left, and that is: life, life; bare, naked, unjustifiable life; just life existing there and for no reason and no end. The end and the reason are for us to say, to project" (692). Cross then shoots Hilton in the temple with the latter's own pistol and leaves a message for Hilton at the front desk, in order to establish an alibi.

Cross is certain Houston will suspect him of killing Hilton, Herndon, and Blount; and, in fact, a police car picks him up after he leaves Hilton's hotel. The police question him about Hilton, but he acts as though he thinks Hilton is still alive. After the police lose interest in questioning Cross as a suspect in Hilton's murder, Houston begins interrogating him. Later, back at Eva's apartment, in a desire to spill everything, Cross confesses that he killed Hilton, that his name is Cross Damon, that he killed her husband and Herndon, and that he killed a man named Joe Thomas, but Eva thinks Cross is just sick. After she gets in bed with him and they make love, Cross considers killing Eva: "Would it not be better for her to die now and be spared the pain and shock which he knew he had to bring yet to her?" (723–24). Cross now realizes that human existence cannot withstand the pressure of too much intellect: "No matter how hot and furious the degree of his thinking, he could not convince himself that to kill Eva to ward off the suffering that the future would bring into the world was right" (724).

As the story continues, Cross and Eva agree to move in with Sarah in Harlem, after which point Menti comes to Sarah's apartment with money from the party for Eva. Explaining to Eva that the party simply wants her to paint, he tells her he will pick her up the next morning and take her to the union hall. But this is not the last we will see of Menti today. Once Menti leaves, Eva gives Cross her diaries to read; he is humiliated because he has already read parts of them. Meanwhile, the party watches Cross 24 hours a day now.

After Eva and Cross return to Sarah's apartment late that evening from a midnight movie, a slightly tipsy Sarah also returns, with Menti, a thug named Hank, and Blimin in tow, the last of whom, Sarah tells Cross, has been asking all about him. Blimin acknowledges to Cross that if he does not clear himself of suspicion in the murders of Gil, Herndon, and Hilton, the Communist Party will take measures to see that he does not remain longer in its midst. Then Blimin angrily demands that Cross share details about his life, which occasions a long speech by Cross on how industrialization is more important than ideology; he also discusses atheism, materialism, and religion. Cross explains to Blimin that the desire for power is what really lies behind fascism and communism.

The next morning, Menti and Hank take Cross, Eva, and Sarah to the union hall so they can pay their respects to Gil. Blimin tells Cross that the party wants to know what Cross wants. Book Four ends when Cross goes to a restaurant to meet Houston for dinner but is instead met by two detectives who disarm him and deliver him to Houston.

The final book of *The Outsider*, "Decision," begins with Cross's realization that he "wantonly violated every commitment that civilized men owe, in terms of common honesty and sacred honor, to those with whom they live" (772). Houston knows by now that Cross worked as a postal clerk in Chicago until a month and a half ago. A man from the post office identifies Cross, and Houston tells Cross that it is believed that his mother just died of shock upon hearing the news that Cross pretended to be dead. Cross takes the position that a man "who believes that he cannot live by the articles of faith of his society is a criminal and you [Houston] know it, even though Congress has not gotten around to making such into law" (785). To break Cross's spirit, Houston has Gladys and her three sons appear in his office, causing Cross to see an "expression of sensual excitement upon the hunchback's face" (786). After Gladys and the boys leave, the district attorney admits that the Communists have been badgering him to take action against Cross for killing Blount, Herndon, and Hilton. Nevertheless, Houston tells Cross that, for the time being, he is free to go.

Cross returns to Sarah's apartment, and Eva meets him there. She is now frightened of Cross, whom the Communists have told her is married. Cross again admits to Eva that he killed Gil and Herndon, explaining that in the former instance, it was not because of her. Eva runs into Sarah's living room and locks the door, at which point Menti and Hank show up. Soon after, Eva commits suicide by jumping out a window in Sarah's apartment.

Planning to escape as quickly as possible, Cross searches for Eva's diaries only to discover that they have been stolen. Just as Cross starts to pack his suitcase, Houston arrives at Sarah's apartment. He proclaims that he knows Cross killed Blount, Herndon, and Hilton; he also has Eva's diaries. Houston reveals that his first real clue that Cross was the murderer was what the latter had been reading in Chicago: Nietzsche, Hegel, Jaspers, Heidegger, Husserl, Kierkegaard, Dostoyevsky—philosophers who wallow in guilty thought, according to Houston. And reading Eva's diaries convinced Houston that it was not desire for Eva that led him to kill. Finally, when Cross stared so unfeelingly at his own sons, Houston knew then that Cross was "beyond the pale of all the *little* feelings, the *humble feelings*, the *human* feelings. . . . I [Houston] *knew that you* [Cross] *could do anything*" (823). Realizing that he could not get a conviction, because he has no concrete evidence, Houston decides to let Cross go free: Cross made his own law, and Houston is going to let him live by it.

After Houston leaves Sarah's apartment and Cross gets some sleep, Cross reads more from Eva's diaries, which Houston had left behind. The entries indicate Eva's sorrow for "Lionel Lane" when she first met him. Sarah then returns to the apartment and informs Cross that she wants him to leave; when he does, Menti and Hank follow him for the rest of the day. He asks his landlady Hattie, who is worried about losing her house, if he can hide at her place, and she agrees when he gives her the $250 she needs to retain ownership. Later, as Cross is about to flee in a taxi, he is shot by Hank or Menti. At the hospital, Cross confesses to Houston that he also killed Joe Thomas. When Houston asks Cross what he has discovered about living as an outsider, Cross replies, "Alone a man is nothing. . . . Man is a promise that he must never break" (839). Just before he dies, Cross tells Houston that what was most horrible about his life is that he is, or feels he is, innocent.

CHARACTER DEVELOPMENT

Of the numerous characters in *The Outsider,* only a handful figure prominently in Wright's novel: the titular protagonist, Cross Damon; Gladys, his wife; Ely Houston, the district attorney; and Eva Blount, the woman Cross falls in love with in the course of the novel. Cross himself (the demon on the cross) is by far the most important character in the book. Overwhelmed by marital problems and burdened with a pregnant, underaged girlfriend, he takes advantage of a subway accident to engage in a philosophical experiment: to what extent can a person ignore social restraints and be self-defining? Except for some feeling for his three sons and his love for Eva, Cross is indifferent or hostile to other people and their rights; he kills and lies at will until he comes up against a political organization that uses the same tactics against him. What he learns is that while there may be no ultimate authority behind social conventions, they are nevertheless the glue that holds the human world together, and thus, however arbitrary, of crucial significance. Although Cross's blackness does reinforce his outsiderness, it is not a decisive factor in his alienation because Cross's character would have been very much the same even if he had not been a person of color. He is almost completely isolated from society per se, although he does have intimate relationships with women throughout the novel. Another element in his character is his philosophical bent: he enjoys theorizing about society, economics, and politics. His master principle seems to be that everything comes down to the issue of power: behind all ideological squabble, Cross finds the real concern to be the question of who will be in control, which is exhibited in his own personal life, as he treats everyone but Eva pretty much as he pleases. Cross crosses boundaries, but not crossing them is how they are maintained. His characterization asks, What is excessive? How far outside norms can one go? The outsiders of the world answer these questions by going outside socially sanctioned limits, a gesture that reestablishes their power and importance. How well Cross as a literary character meshes with Cross as a literary philosopher is an open question.

Cross's estranged wife, Gladys, is characterized in more race-based terms than is her husband, as she went to an integrated school, where she experienced racial prejudice from the white students. A nurse, mother, and wife, she is depicted by Wright as a black woman who deserves far better than what she receives from Cross Damon, who tends to regard her more and more as a burden he needs to unload. She proves to be a strong and determined person after he feigns madness, and thus she complicates the view of Wright's attitude toward black women that is based on Bessie Mears and Mrs. Thomas in *Native Son*. She stands by their three sons and endures the painful scene toward the end of *The Outsider* when Cross, for the most part, remains remote from his family, which Ely Houston has brought to New York to confront him.

Serving as Cross's double in *The Outsider*, Ely Houston is an outsider on the inside who knows what Cross knows but remains within the lines of what society tolerates. As a man with a physical deformity, as a hunchback, Houston is characterized as one who understands Cross's racial separateness; neither chose the social liabilities with which he was born, but both are nevertheless held responsible for them. However, Houston is also Cross's secret philosophical duplicate. If Houston is Cross's double, then Cross is also Houston's, and Houston is thus fascinated by this man who acts on his beliefs rather than just analyzes them, as Houston himself does. He is also depicted as a man who relishes the search for the murderer of Gil Blount, Langley Herndon, and Jack Hilton and who takes a sadistic pleasure in watching Cross's temporary discomfort when confronted by his family. But he does sympathize with and understand Cross; in letting Cross go free, he is not only partially responsible for his death, but he also denies his double any social acknowledgment of his own contempt for social norms.

Eva Blount is the one person in *The Outsider* whom Cross loves. She has been used by the Communist Party to serve as Gil's wife, although he is completely indifferent to her feelings. She is Eve-like in that she is not suspicious of others until forced to be; but when she learns more about Cross than she can accept, she commits suicide. She paints abstract pictures that are neither understood nor appreciated by her fellow Communists. She is little more than a victim preyed upon by the men in her life, as well as by the political institution into which she placed her trust.

THEMATIC ISSUES

Several basic thematic concepts preside over *The Outsider*, the most salient of which is suggested by the title itself: outsiderness. The protagonist resides in a space that lies outside what social conventions underwrite: restraint, law, self-control, respect for others. Acknowledging no law higher than himself, he does not understand until his death that even if this is a defensible position, no society can tolerate a Cross Damon, for there would be no society if he were tolerated. Granting society and others no rights, Cross cannot reasonably expect them to grant him any either. Wright's interest here is determining what the effects will be of someone who turns his back on all social obligations. Conventions, the glue that holds society together, may be arbitrary, but they are necessary, Wright seems to suggest and Cross Damon seems to understand at his death; they enable and sustain human relations that would otherwise be impossible.

Closely tied to the issue of outsiderness is the theme of identity, of who Cross is. From one perspective, he is anyone he cares to be: Cross Damon, Charles Webb, Addison Jordan, Lionel Lane. In other words, identity is like choosing a part in a play: you choose whatever role you care to play in any given performance of the play. But from another vantage point, identity is a responsibility and a function of social relations: Cross is a father of three boys and one unborn child, although he rejects fatherhood; he is Gladys's husband, although he rejects that role, too. But by himself, Cross is not anything (he remarks to Houston that "man is nothing in particular"), because identity, Wright suggests, is an effect of society, and since Cross is not part of society, he has no identity. He needs society far more than it needs him. Cross wants what society offers, but he does not want to make the compromises that it demands. Over society's expectations, he chooses extreme personal autonomy.

It is this issue of personal autonomy that leads Wright to explore another area of concern in *The Outsider*, communism. Earlier in his life, Wright had seen communism as a real possibility for solving social problems, but his experience in the Communist Party caused him to reject it. In *The Outsider* it is depicted as ruthless, bureaucratic, aggressive, cynical, as anything but a visionary revolutionary movement. It is interested in Cross Damon only because he is black; it arranges a loveless marriage for Eva Blount; it spies on Cross and has him murdered. It is interested in the accumulation of power for power's sake, something Wright found particularly objectionable because that is what he faced in the South when he was growing up there. There is, in other words, no personal freedom in the Communist Party in Wright's view, as it was expressed in this novel.

AN ALTHUSSERIAN READING

Although *The Outsider* reveals profound doubts about Marxism as practiced in the form of twentieth-century communism, it can nevertheless be approached from the point of view of one of Marx's most provocative interpreters, Louis Althusser, the French writer and critic who argues that what a group of people think of as given or natural is actually a disguise for the relation between the ruling class and its subjects, the workers. Since the ruling class exploits the workers, as Marx and Althusser hold, this relation has to be hidden under ideology for it to survive. The workers, the subjects, are given definition by being "hailed" or "recruited" (Althusser often uses the term "interpellated") by what Althusser refers to as "Ideological State Apparatuses," or ISAs, which social systems use to repress and control their members. Examples of ISAs would include the family, churches, clubs, the law, political parties, trade unions, newspapers, literature—basically, any entity that the ruling class, or its agent, the state, uses to subject and dominate the working class. In fact, Althusser contends that the workers do not have individual identities until they are recruited by ISAs, until they are hailed by ISAs. What the working class regards as natural, Althusser regards as exploitation. Ideology is the system by which the ruling class disguises the subordinate relation of the working class to the factory owners; it makes the imaginary seem real, according to Althusser.

From Althusser's point of view, then, what is driving Cross Damon to extremes is his sense that the social institutions that offer him an identity are only ISAs, or different ways to control him and the other people in his life. The institutions of marriage and the family, for instance, hail Cross as a father and a husband, when he wants to be a sexual opportunist. He rejects the ideology of marriage in favor of pursuing various women to whom he is not married. The post office, where Cross works, is another instrument, from Althusser's vantage point, used by the state to give Cross an identity and to subject him to its whims. Even the informal drinking club Cross belongs to, comprised of his friends from the post office, is just another diversion from the reality of Cross's life that he is merely an exploited worker.

The Communist Party itself would be the most salient example of an ISA in the novel, in that it is represented by Wright as the insatiable desire for power that requires new members only for the sake of increasing its power. What happens to Bob Hunter at the hands of the party is a result of the workings of an entity that its leaders want to become an apparatus of the state. Similarly, what gives Cross's mother a sense of identity is the church she attends, an institution Althusser would also cite as an example of an ISA, as he would the Catholic Church to which Sarah Hunter returns at the end of *The Outsider.* Even the integrated school Gladys attended, the legal system Ely Houston heads, and the painting Eva does (a cultural ISA) can all be observed as means of state control that enable the rule of the wealthy, in Althusser's view. From an Althusserian perspective, *The Outsider* questions the values of social institutions.

7

Eight Men
(1961)

Eight Men is a posthumously published collection of five short stories, two radio plays, and one autobiographical essay, the latter of which also appears in the 1991 unexpurgated version of *Black Boy*, and thus it is not discussed here. The two radio plays had not been previously published, but the other items had appeared at various times over Wright's career, beginning in 1937 in the case of "The Man Who Saw the Flood," originally published under the title "Silt." Each piece, as the title of the collection says, explores the issue of manhood, a particularly sensitive issue in the black community. The definitions and styles of manhood vary greatly, from Carl's cross-dressing in "Man of All Work" to Tom's more traditional form of devotedness to family in "The Man Who Saw the Flood."

"THE MAN WHO WAS ALMOST A MAN"

PLOT DEVELOPMENT

The plot of the opening story in the collection, "The Man Who Was Almost a Man," is simple and effective: 17-year-old Dave Saunders, who plows fields for the local plantation owner, Jim Hawkins, is dissatisfied with his status in the world. To leapfrog into manhood, he determines to buy a gun from a store owner named Joe. With a gun, Dave is certain he will command the respect and power adolescent males crave. The day after buying it, he takes it with him to the field he is plowing in order to fire it, but he "accidentally" shoots and kills Mr. Hawkins's mule, Jenny. No one believes Dave's lie that she fell on the point of a plow; worse, a crowd of blacks and whites laughs at him as his mother gets the truth out of him and his father says he plans to beat him. Further, he now owes Mr. Hawkins $50 for a dead mule.

Early the next morning, Dave retrieves the gun from where he had buried it and fires the four remaining cartridges, wishing afterward that he had saved one to fire at Mr. Hawkins's plantation. At the story's end, he jumps a freight train headed north (where the racial attitudes of the South will still exist), certain he is bound for manhood.

CHARACTER DEVELOPMENT

Dave's character is the most fully developed in the story. He is bitterly frustrated by his lack of authority and power: he plows the fields for their white owner, Jim Hawkins; his mother receives his pay directly from his boss; he lives with his brother and parents; he is only 17. These frustrations are further complicated by the fact that Dave Saunders is black. But a black male with a gun, he thinks, is someone to be respected, by parents, other blacks, and whites. Dave conflates, though, a symbol of respect with respect itself, and in misusing this symbol, he accidentally shoots an innocent animal as opposed to the real target of his frustration, Mr. Hawkins himself. The other characters—his parents, Jim Hawkins, and Joe—are only sketched in, as they serve as foils to Dave.

THEMATIC ISSUES

A central concern in "The Man Who Was Almost a Man," as is suggested by the title of the collection and by the titles of this and the other stories in it, is "manhood," one of the most loaded terms in the English language. It is a term with particular resonance for the African American community, because its men have traditionally been denied manhood by the dominant culture. If, as a provisional definition, the term can be thought of as the maximization of options, then most black men, until recently, have not had access to it because they have been denied so many options. Dave Saunders himself has very limited choices: he can continue plowing Mr. Hawkins's fields and be a kind of human version of the mule Jenny, or he can go north; he chooses the latter. He has mistaken an emblem of power, a gun, for power (that is, opportunity) itself. Had he fired his gun at Mr. Hawkins's plantation as he wished he had done, he would quickly have found out how powerless he was, if he had been caught.

Related to the issue of masculinity is the theme of growing up: like any adolescent male, Dave is frustrated by social controls, such as his family, that restrict his freedom. The oxymoronic title of the story (how can a man be almost a man?) accurately conveys Dave's frustration, one with which any teenaged male can readily identify.

A FREUDIAN READING

The Austrian psychiatrist Sigmund Freud contended that we have a lively subconscious that contains all sorts of fantasies and desires that social pressure causes us to repress. The most notorious example is what Freud named the "Oedipus complex," the belief that sons harbor secret desires of usurping their father's sexual position in the family structure. In Dave Saunders's case, it does not require much effort to see that he is indeed repressing certain desires and that he believes his frustration can somehow be allayed with the use of a traditional symbol of male power, a gun, which has obvious phallic significance. Thus, his handling of it, keeping it tied to his thigh, and its size and weight might suggest a Freudian interpretation of adolescent obsession with masturbation. To turn in another Freudian direction, Dave's supposedly unintentional killing of Jenny implies his hatred of being a human mule, a beast of burden that plows the fields all day. Since Dave cannot kill the system that oppresses him, he shoots a symbol of it—a female symbol, too, Freud might point out.

"THE MAN WHO LIVED UNDERGROUND"

The longest, and to many readers, most remarkable story in *Eight Men,* "The Man Who Lived Underground," was first published in the early 1940s, when the whole world was being menaced by the ultimate underground man, Adolf Hitler, who is alluded to in Wright's story in the figure of a butcher with a Hitlerian mustache. By taking the protagonist Fred Daniels on a nightmarish journey through the underworld of twentieth-century America, Wright makes it clear that he understood the constructedness of human values decades before this idea became so prominent in the humanities. In fact, Fred is eventually killed by a policeman with the suggestive name of Lawson because the latter says the Fred Daniels of this world would wreck things (by pointing out the challengeability of human values). In other words, Fred is a threat to societies because he has learned that their values are human inventions and not natural.

PLOT DEVELOPMENT

"The Man Who Lived Underground" begins with the protagonist hiding in the sewer system of an unidentified U.S. city in order to escape from the police, who have forced him to confess to a crime he did not commit. What he observes and experiences underground takes up most of the plot, which includes, most notably, his observing a church service and his seeing an aborted fetus. The black congregation in the church is "[j]ust singing with the air of the sewer blowing in on them" (24). The dead baby has been flushed down the toilet, but it is what the aboveground society wants to flush away that Fred sees or smells or touches in the sewer. After peeking at a corpse in an undertaker's establishment, he enters a movie theater, where he views the audience as "children, sleeping in their living, awake in their dying" (30). He soon afterward takes a radio from a radio shop and then watches a butcher in a meat market: "The man's face was hard, square, grim; a jet of mustache smudged his upper lip and a glistening cowlick of hair fell over his left eye" (38). This description and the date of first publication of "The Man Who Lived Underground," 1942 (during World War II), point unmistakably toward Hitler as the reference, as he was indeed a butcher.

Given the opportunity to rob a safe of its money and diamonds, Daniels does so, not because he wants to spend the money or because he covets diamonds, but because of the sensation and because he will not be punished. In a sewer, money has no value and neither do diamonds. Wright is structuring the plot to indicate the conventionality of aboveground values. Back in a dirt cave he has constructed for himself, the protagonist cannot remember his name, another indication of the arbitrariness upon which the world above the sewer is based. Tapping into some exposed electrical wiring to supply current to a lightbulb, he also dabs glue onto the wall and uses the money to wallpaper his cave. The sense of triumph over the aboveground world is exhilarating, but he does not stop with using money as wallpaper: he also flings the diamonds over the floor of his cave. "Maybe *anything's* right, he mumbled. Yes, if the world as men had made it was right, then anything else was right, any act a man took to satisfy himself, murder, theft, torture" (56). Certainly, a strong case can be made that Daniels's thought has been acted on by many people in the twentieth century.

The plot resumes in the world of sunshine with Daniels determined to tell the policemen who forced a confession out of him about his recent underworld experiences, but the effort results only in his being murdered by the one with the ironic name of Lawson. Asked why he shot Daniels, Lawson says, "You've got to shoot his kind. They'd wreck things"(84), meaning by "his kind" people who have come to understand the arbitrariness of the surface world's values, who are therefore a threat to that world.

CHARACTER DEVELOPMENT

The only character in "The Man Who Lived Underground" who is developed at all is the protagonist, Fred Daniels, but this may well be appropriate, considering that the story is a philosophical allegory (a symbolic representation of truths about human existence). In such a genre, concepts and abstractions occupy the center of the reader's interest, not fully developed characters. Fred Daniels is more or less the average person, who in this case has been wrongfully accused of a murder. His view of the world is profoundly altered by his underworld journey, because it causes him to see that what he took seriously, the sunshine world, had its absurd side just underneath the surface.

THEMATIC ISSUES

"The Man Who Lived Underground" is one of Wright's most suggestive works of fiction, woven of numerous thematic strands, including the lower world versus the upper world, the underground man, and the

United States as a sewer. Fred Daniels's underground adventures help him understand the conventionality of aboveground values: he eventually forgets his name, a social convenience back on the surface but useless in the sewer (he once types it in lowercase letters and without a space as "freddaniels"). Because money and diamonds have no exchange value underground, they may as well be used for decoration and be trampled into the dirt. What the sunshine world takes as given or natural, the dark world reveals to be arbitrary. In the sewer world, Fred Daniels "sees"; aboveground, where he had eyes and light, he was "in the dark."

Daniels exemplifies a long-standing tradition in colonial America and U.S. history: the underground man versus man as a social being. As the man who lived underground, Daniels is autonomous and isolated, but he wants to tell someone of his experiences, which is fatal. Society kills, Wright implies, but total isolation is unbearable. U.S. culture has never resolved the tension between the desire to be an autonomous individual and the desire for social interaction. Unlike Robinson Crusoe, Fred Daniels never finds a Friday, a companion. And when he does try to reenter society, he is perceived as a threat. Daniels's underground vision is dark indeed, but not because there is no sunlight in the sewer system. The fetus that floats by him perhaps most disturbingly suggests what the surface world is about: flush what is unwanted down the toilet, because it will not be seen that way. But Daniels encounters what the surface world flushes away; he even wades around in it. He lives amid the waste of twentieth-century U.S. civilization, which does not want to know what is right underneath it, any more than the churchgoers he observes realize "the air of the sewer [is] blowing in on them" (24). And yet it is the world built on a sewer that judges him guilty, even though he did not commit the crime he is accused of perpetrating.

AN INTERTEXTUAL READING

Placing Wight's story next to other literary versions of the underworld journey can illuminate both. Visits to the underworld are frequent in the Western literary tradition: in *Gilgamesh* (an ancient Mesopotamian epic), *The Odyssey* (an ancient Greek epic attributed to Homer), *The Aeneid* (an unfinished Roman epic by Virgil), and *The Divine Comedy* (a medieval epic by Dante). The protagonists of these tales also undertake journeys to the underworld, like Fred Daniels does in "The Man Who Lived Underground." Yet these four versions of the underground motif differ in revealing ways from Wright's. For instance, in *Gilgamesh* (the word itself means "the old man becomes a young man"), the hero is said to be two-thirds divine and one-third human, and he undertakes a search for immortality that involves his being given a boxthorn plant, which a snake steals from him. In *The Odyssey*, during his visit to the underworld, Osysseus sees his mother and various other Greek figures, including Achilles, the greatest of the Greek warriors who fought in the Trojan War. Virgil's hero encounters the woman he rejected, Dido, who turns her back on him, and his father, who reveals to him that his destiny is to found the Roman Empire. In Dante's version of the journey, the poet himself, led by Virgil, sees many figures, both from his time (Dante lived from 1265 to 1321) and from the past, suffering in hell in ways that fit their earthly crimes.

Fred Daniels's journey underground, however, is secular: he does not encounter any spirits, and he is not looking for immortality. He himself is an ordinary mortal, not someone of mythological or historical stature. Nor is his journey underground nationalistic; on the contrary, what he sees suggests a civilization resting on a sewer. In fact, Fred Daniels's underworld experiences may suggest why humankind is so attached to religion and nationalism: they provide the satisfaction that reality lacks, and all Daniels sees, at least from Wright's perspective, is reality. His reward for his underground experiences is not immortality or national heroism, but death at the hands of the policeman Lawson. "The Man Who Lived Underground" rejects its predecessors; it is an anti-epic, more in line with *Notes from the Underground*, by the nineteenth-century Russian novelist Fyodor Dostoyevsky, and with *Invisible Man*, by the twentieth-century African American novelist Ralph Ellison. "The Man Who Lived Underground" is a provocative and extended literary conversation with both its predecessors and its successors.

"BIG BLACK GOOD MAN"

PLOT DEVELOPMENT

Originally published in 1957, "Big Black Good Man" uses a straightforward plot that is based on the central character's misperception regarding a physically imposing black man named Jim, who may be Wright's correction of Mark Twain's passive, humble Jim in *Huckleberry Finn*. The main character, Olaf Jensen, works as a night porter in a cheap waterfront hotel in Copenhagen, which caters to sailors looking for lodging, whiskey, and prostitutes. Musing about his life the night before he turns 60, Olaf wishes he and his wife had had children, but then he tells himself that his tenants are his children. A "huge black thing" (87), as Olaf perceives it, fills his doorway; this "thing" is a human being who happens to be large and black, Jim. His physical appearance alone is Jim's "mistake," in an echo of the same "mistake" Rodney King (the black man who was severely beaten by members of the Los Angeles Police Department in 1993) and other black men have apparently shared across time. In response to Jim's request for a whore, Olaf provides Lena, who always gives him a 15 percent cut of what she charges instead of the usual 10 percent. After her first night with Jim, Olaf asks Lena how it was, to which she inquires whether Olaf wants to take over her work. The plot's first climax occurs when Jim puts his fingers around Olaf's throat in an action that Olaf misinterprets (Jim is determining Olaf's collar size): Olaf "lost control of the reflexes of his body and he felt a hot stickiness flooding his underwear" (96), apparently meaning diarrhea or possibly some other bodily fluid. Olaf is resolved to kill Jim if he sees him again, but after a year elapses without Jim's reappearance, Olaf assumes he will not see him again.

When Jim does reappear, we experience a second climax: almost ready to shoot Jim with a gun he keeps in a drawer, Olaf realizes the black sailor means only to give him the six white shirts he was measuring him for when Olaf soiled himself. There is no need for Olaf to try to get Lena for Jim, because they have been writing each other and Jim is going to her house. It finally hits Olaf that Jim likes him and never intended him any harm. Olaf was afraid of an assumption that he had internalized—that large black men are homicidal maniacs—whereas Jim has no connection to such an idea.

CHARACTER DEVELOPMENT

Olaf and Jim are ordinary human beings, which is part of Wright's point in the story. The most significant difference between them is that until the end of the story, Olaf reacts to "Jim," not to Jim, which is to say that Olaf sees what he believes rather than what actually exists. Olaf sees something that lives only in his racist fantasies rather than the truth that Jim is just a human being, who happens to be black, male, and large. There is nothing particularly noteworthy about Jim. Olaf could not be much more ordinary himself: he is married, has a vegetable garden, has poor eyesight, and is five feet seven inches tall. But even when he sees better in the figurative sense, he still sees a big black good man, not a good big black man. Jim misperceives Olaf also, not realizing he is hated and feared by him, although Jim likes Olaf, as his generous tip and the six white shirts prove. Lena, too, is just an ordinary human being, who supports herself through prostitution and is indifferent to Jim's skin color and size.

THEMATIC ISSUES

The title of this short story itself performs considerable thematic work: the word "big" is one Wright uses in association with black males elsewhere, too, as in Bigger Thomas (who is five feet nine inches tall) and Big Boy Morrison in "Big Boy Leaves Home." Large black men, such as Rodney King, are still sometimes perceived as threats, whereas they are just human beings who happen to be large, black, and male. But as Wright knew all too well, reality can be replaced by racist preconceptions, as it is in "Big Black Good Man."

The story is also deeply concerned with vision: for one thing, what we see is largely restricted to Olaf's point of view. As a product of racial bias, Olaf has "preseen" Jim. That is to say, he sees what he believes when he sees Jim—that physically imposing black men are a threat (historically speaking, white men have been the threat to black men). For another thing, Wright repeatedly emphasizes Olaf's poor eyesight to reinforce the theme of seeing in the sense of understanding.

What helps put these ideas across to the reader is the humor in "Big Black Good Man." Wright's sly racial humor works well here, as this time it is the white man who is worried, however needlessly, about black male power. Readers may also smile when Olaf soils himself as Jim takes his neck measurement because he wants to give him some shirts, but

Olaf fears his neck is about to be snapped! This is one case of racial mis-understanding in Wright's work that does not lead to violence.

A FEMINIST READING

From the point of view of female readers, "Big Black Good Man" may be Lena's story more than Olaf's or Jim's, especially if feminism is thought of as awareness of compassion and sensitivity rather than obsession with physicality in matters of heterosexuality. Olaf is proud that he grew the biggest carrots of anybody and also concerned about Jim's sexuality in terms of physical dimensions, but to Lena a male customer is just that, a customer, a financial transaction. It is when she gets to know Jim personally that she values him as more than a source of money. For her, the physical side of sex is merely physical and commercial; it is Jim's kindness that apparently attracts her on a more permanent and personal basis. Olaf, on the other hand, conceives of heterosexuality largely in terms of whether or not it results in children (an outward sign of his manhood) and in terms of physical size. He thinks of it only in a patriarchal manner, which the story humorously undermines. The means to sexual fulfillment is kindness and humor, not mere physicality.

"THE MAN WHO SAW THE FLOOD"

PLOT DEVELOPMENT

The plot of "The Man Who Saw the Flood," which was published originally under the title "Silt" in 1937, is slight but effective. It is based on the return of a family of black sharecroppers to what is left of their home after a flood. So little is left that the reader marvels at the family's determination to start over: "A dresser sat cater-cornered, its drawers and sides bulging like a bloated corpse. The bed, with the mattress still on it, was like a giant casket forged of mud" (104). The family takes understandable hope from the fact that the floodwaters left a box of matches and a half-full sack of tobacco untouched. When Tom, the father, decides he had better see the white man who owns the land about starting over with a new stake, the latter drives up in his buggy and tells Tom to get in. The plot ends on a slightly upbeat note, as Tom's wife yells to him to bring back some molasses for his daughter.

CHARACTER DEVELOPMENT

The characters of this story are sketched in somewhat slightly because Wright's interest is in the ability of a black family as a unit to persevere, not in individual characters. Tom is a sharecropper devoted to his wife, May, and their daughter, Sally. The three are clearly used to functioning as a tight-knit unit, especially when under pressure. They rent the land from Burgess, a white man who has an economic stranglehold on them. Confronted by a hostile nature and an equally hostile economic system, this black family is too strong to give up.

THEMATIC ISSUES

Perhaps the central theme in "The Man Who Saw the Flood" is the profound respect Wright has for this family of sharecroppers. Not all of Wright's families are dysfunctional, as this one demonstrates. Caught in the crop-lien system—meaning that they rent the land, the mule, the fertilizer, and the seed from Burgess and then repay him with their harvest, should they have one—they are resigned to live a life of struggle. When a flood nearly destroys what little they have in their rented cabin, they still stay together and try again, although they owe Burgess $800, a considerable sum of money in the early part of the twentieth century, when the story is apparently set. Wright is celebrating a traditional, nuclear black family here, and he is indicting the system that holds such families down.

A MARXIST READING

It is not easy to resist a Marxist reading of "The Man Who Saw the Flood" because it embodies the classic target of Marxist analysis: a group of workers exploited by capitalism. Certainly Marx, and Wright in 1937, would have concurred that a revolutionary overthrow of people like Burgess would have been the only solution to the problems with which the black family in the story is burdened. The crop-lien system will keep this family in perpetual debt to Burgess, who can continue to profit from their physical labor simply because he owns the land. While they retain their dignity, he retains them. Such a system must be overthrown if the people it exploits are to have a real chance at happiness in this world.

"MAN OF ALL WORK"

PLOT DEVELOPMENT

The next piece in *Eight Men*, a radio play titled "Man of All Work" that had not been published before, is based on a plot that turns on the central male character's passing as a black woman for six hours to earn enough money to enable his family to keep its house. Carl, an unemployed professional cook, has a wife (Lucy), a young son (Henry), and a week-old daughter (Tina) to support, but the restaurant he cooked for has gone out of business. If they do not find the money for their last two mortgage payments, they will lose their house. Carl comes across a classified ad for a job as a combination cook/housekeeper that he decides he must try to get, as he is not qualified for any other job, but the position requires a female applicant.

When Lucy insists that Carl not impersonate a woman just to get this job, he assures her that he was just joking. Nevertheless, Carl indeed goes to the white family that placed the ad, the Fairchilds, which lost its last maid because of Mr. Fairchild's alcohol-induced sexual advances toward her, and successfully applies for the position.

Employed by the Fairchilds, Carl/Lucy (he takes his wife's name for his female persona) has no difficulty fooling Mr. And Mrs. Fairchild into thinking that he is a woman, but their daughter, Lily, notices that Carl/Lucy's arms "are so big" (125). Dave Fairchild, the father, has a drink and proceeds to pressure Carl/Lucy, who has just been ordered to wash Mrs. Fairchild's back while she bathes, for sex. Anne Fairchild, the mother, comes upon the two with a gun and shoots Carl/Lucy in the thigh, an incident with sexual overtones. At this, Anne's brother-in-law, Burt Stallman, is called to the Fairchilds' house because he is a doctor. In giving Carl/Lucy medical attention, Burt discovers the truth, that Carl/Lucy is actually a man. In exchange for $200, which will pay off Carl's mortgage and leave money for food, Carl promises to say nothing about what really happened at the Fairchilds' house. When he finally gets home after such a day, Carl exclaims to his wife, "I was a woman for six hours and it almost killed me" (154).

CHARACTER DEVELOPMENT

The main figures in the triangle of "Man of All Work"— Carl, Dave Fairchild, and Anne Fairchild—are the only characters developed to any appreciable extent. The central question in Carl's case is whether he is Carl (which in Scots means a stout, manly fellow), or Lucy, or both. In other words, in a society that insists on policing gender boundaries, on which side of the line is Carl? Wright's answer seems to be that what matters is that Carl is willing to do anything for his family, regardless of whether that makes him masculine, feminine, or both. Carl's most important character trait is that unlike some of Wright's characterizations of fathers, he is unconditionally devoted to his wife and children. He is also as skillful at caring for his children as their mother is, as Wright illustrates when Carl burps Tina.

In contrast to Carl as a devoted family man, Dave Fairchild is characterized as a sexual predator who takes advantage of black women and a man who has problems with alcohol. His wife worries about her weight and whether her husband will treat Carl/Lucy the same way he treated Bertha, the previous maid. The Fairchilds are not fair children at all, but rather privileged white people who can afford to pay hush money to avoid a public confrontation with the scandalous truth of their lives.

THEMATIC ISSUES

Wright raises some particularly provocative thematic issues in "Man of All Work": gender as it is related to outward appearance, the nature of work, and what constitutes a "home." A black man dressing like a woman is an especially sensitive issue because of the intense concern about manhood in African American experience: if dress determines gender, then Carl/Lucy is a woman. If anatomy determines gender, then Carl/Lucy is a man. If role determines gender, then Carl/Lucy is a woman and a man, because he both nurtures his children and will do anything to ensure their financial support. He remarks to his wife that "colored men are now wearing their hair long. . . . Look at Sugar Ray Robinson's [a gifted black boxer in the 1950s] hair. Look at Nat King Cole's [a popular black singer in the 1950s and 1960s] hair. Look at all the colored men in the Black Belt. They straighten their hair. It's the style" (116). Can a man, particularly a black man, wear his hair long and still be a *black man*? Wright's answer in "Man of All Work" is in the affirmative. Strength of character, not gender, dress, or hairstyle, determines manhood for Wright.

A second thematic concern explored in the story is the supposed provisionality of the black family. But the traditional, nuclear black family the reader sees is stronger than ever at the story's conclusion: its house, which is also its home, will soon be paid for, the parents are both present and happily married, and they have two kids; there is no doubt that both parents will soon be working again. Social pathology in this story has infected the white family, which has the money to hide its condition from society.

A CULTURAL READING

Cultural criticism resists the authority of a society's assumptions by subjecting them to analytical questioning. What is taken for granted, about social or sexual orientation, for instance, is made available for examination and challenged. That women are suitable for only certain jobs would be an example of an idea that is increasingly unacceptable in the United States. Or the belief that happiness for women lies only in a heterosexual relationship within the institution of marriage would be something else that is increasingly being rethought. The implications of such an approach for "Man of All Work" are quite suggestive. If men are not supposed to wear dresses and yet Carl believes he must wear one in order to support his family, where does his belief leave the gender-based dress code? Wright also questions whether women are the nurturers and men the providers, because Carl is very maternal toward his baby and, although a provider, he earns money for his family by performing work traditionally associated with black women. Wright seems to be implying that gendered roles are not natural or given, but mere social arrangements that can be recontextualized. What he himself does not reconsider is whether or not a family can be made up only of heterosexual parents and their biological children: both the black and the white families in the story are so configured as to leave that notion intact. Also challenged, though, is the belief that black men are obsessed with a narrow definition of masculinity. Carl will do anything for his family, for it is his family that he prizes, not the world's opinion of him or its insistence on judging him from some narrowly conceived set of assumptions.

"MAN, GOD AIN'T LIKE THAT"

PLOT DEVELOPMENT

The plot of the other radio play in *Eight Men*, "Man, God Ain't Like That," pivots around the conflict between an African named Babu and a U.S. painter named John Franklin (who, in pursuing his career in Paris, recalls another Franklin who also pursued his career in Paris, while wearing a coonskin cap). Franklin and his wife, Elsie, are traveling in Africa when the car he is driving in a storm hits Babu, causing a head wound. After getting him medical attention, the couple thinks it would be droll to take the "exotic" Babu back to Paris with them, where he would wear his robe and be a kind of noble savage. The Franklins do not understand that Babu thinks John is like Jesus, nor do they grasp that John is using Babu as a model of "the African," a chimera. Neither Babu nor John perceives the other as just a human being from a different culture, which is what any human being is.

Back in Paris, and in different cabs, Babu and the Franklins become separated. Over a month later, Babu reappears, declaring that he has "been about his papa's business" (174), an echo of Christ's statement that he had been about his father's business, as well as a reference to Babu's earthly father, whose bones he carries in a suitcase. He announces that he has found a picture of John Franklin when the painter posed as a model for Christ, but Babu thinks Franklin *is* Christ. Babu reasons that if whites killed Christ and were as a result given the ability to build the monuments of European architecture, then if he kills Franklin, blacks will get the same kind of power whites have. Accordingly, Babu decapitates Franklin, but the French police think Franklin's murder was a crime of passion—namely, that Franklin's mistress, Odile DuFour, killed him.

CHARACTER DEVELOPMENT

Two characters in "Man, God Ain't Like That" are developed to some degree, Babu and John Franklin. The painter is a thoroughly obnoxious and self-centered racist, who regards Babu as an amusing but exasperating subhuman, although useful as a model of "the African." He treats his wife according to his moods and is in general an unsympathetic character. Wright depicts Babu as a confused young African who has misconceived Christianity (or has he?) as a religion based on sacrifice rewarded by earthly power and authority. More an opportunity for an analysis of fatal cultural misconstrual than a credible human figure, Babu is developed into a symbol that serves Wright's purposes in the story but is hardly flattering to real African human beings.

THEMATIC ISSUES

"Man, God Ain't Like That" examines several key issues, including Eurocentricity and the difficult problem of how something should be represented. Eurocentricity is the idea that European values are universal: for instance, the Parthenon in Athens is the standard for architecture anywhere anytime, or the ancient statues of nude, young, Greek males are the standard for sculpture anywhere anytime. It is this kind of thinking that has accompanied European imperialism in Africa; the Europeans have forced their values and aesthetics on Africans who have their own Afrocentric values. In Wright's story, Babu has internalized Western notions of "cultural superiority" and attributed them to Christianity. He believes if he kills John Franklin, who he thinks is a latter-day Christ, Africans will have what whites have. Wright felt that in destroying indigenous Africans cultures, Europeans created a vacuum in which bizarre results were likely, because people must believe in something, as Babu demonstrates. The Franklins have no understanding or respect for African culture: they view it and Africans as quaint and exotic. The result is both humorous and grave, as a self-centered painter is mistaken for Christ and beheaded.

Also analyzed in the story is the issue of representation, in particular, the matter of how Christ should be represented. Although no one knows what Christ looked like (there is no description of him in the New Testament), Babu at first thinks John Franklin looks like Jesus because he has seen a picture of the latter in a Sunday school book. Later, Babu is convinced the painter is God because he finds a picture of Christ for which he believes Franklin posed. In other words, Babu has mistaken a representation of a concept (the Christian notion that Christ was God in human form) for the concept itself. He does not distinguish something from the way it is represented, which leads to Franklin's decapitation. The issue of representation is a particularly heated one now, so this story is of special interest to the contemporary reader, as it engages the issue in a shocking way.

A POSTCOLONIALIST READING

Of various kinds of postcolonialist approaches available for reading literature, one type emphasizes the effects on formerly colonized people of foreign domination. It examines the struggle with personal, cultural, and national identity oppressed peoples are left to face after the departure of European power. Babu has apparently grown up in Ghana, a former British colony in west Africa. He is hit by a car driven by John Franklin, an American painter living in Paris who is visiting Africa. In "broken" English, Babu tells the Franklins he learned to sing Christian songs in the "Mission church." He also explains to them that he cut the throats of chickens and "let blood run" to his dead father "to say thanks to God" (162). He is a Methodist but also practices his "tribal religion" (172). At the end of the story, he returns to Africa to organize a new religious cult that includes the idea that John Franklin will return from the dead. From a postcolonial perspective, then, "Man, God Ain't Like That" indicts Western imperialism because it undermines the indigenous culture it colonizes and produces confused adaptations to its values among those who try to assimilate it. Babu has lost his original cultural identity and replaced it with a misbegotten version of Christianity because of Western colonialism. Wright implies that Western colonial policy undermined local culture and generated a deformed version of European culture in its wake.

"THE MAN WHO KILLED A SHADOW"

PLOT DEVELOPMENT

On the surface, the plot of "The Man Who Killed a Shadow" is sensationalistic and violent, because it is based on an extremely brutal murder by the central character, Saul Saunders, of a "shadow" with the perhaps overly suggestive name of Maybelle Eva Houseman. Saul works as a janitor in the National Cathedral in Washington, D.C., where he comes into contact with his victim Maybelle, the librarian at the cathedral. She insists that he clean under her desk, which he does while she exposes her crotch. He responds to her calling him a "black nigger" (193) by slapping her, which results in her screaming continuously. To stop the screaming, he hits her with a piece of firewood, but she continues to yell. He then chokes her to end the screaming, but she still does it, at which point he does stop it by stabbing her in the throat.

CHARACTER DEVELOPMENT

The two main character are studies in repression: Maybelle Eva Houseman, whose first two names suggest an idyllic sexuality perhaps undercut by her last name, is obsessed with the idea of Saul Saunders seeing her crotch. Saul has no sexual interest in her, and, in fact, she dies a virgin. Saul does have repressed rage against the shadowy (that is, unreal) whites who oppress him, but her calling him, interestingly, what might seem a redundant racial epithet causes him to strike out not only at her, but also at what she represents to him: irrational white oppression. The intentional absurdity of the title (how is it possible to kill a shadow?) is justified when the reader comprehends that Saul was unknowingly attacking white racism when he killed the librarian, but unlike his possible namesake, Saul of Tarsus (Paul), he does not have a vision; Maybelle Eva Houseman remains opaque to him. To her, on the other hand, Saul as a black man could meet her sexual needs. Each remains a shadow to the other.

THEMATIC ISSUES

Repression and the connection between racism and sexuality are dominant thematic issues in "The Man Who Killed a Shadow." The librarian is a study in denial: she will not admit to herself that she is attracted to Saul in spite of herself, but she is also a victim of racial prejudice against him; she seems ignorant of her mixed feelings, yet she does behave in an aggressive manner toward her assailant. She does not know herself at all. Nor does her killer know himself either: he senses that the white world is profoundly awry because, otherwise, how can his mistreatment by it be explained? But he does not recognize that in reality white racism is the cause of his anger—he is not killing a shadow when he kills her, but a material representation and individual agent of his oppression. Wright has coupled stereotypes about black male sexuality to racism to convey the concept that although these ideas are shadowy—that is, unsubstantial as ideas—they are nevertheless something that has to be "killed."

A FREUDIAN READING

Freudian readers will never hit bottom in "The Man Who Killed a Shadow." The Austrian psychiatrist held that people repress their most unsettling desires because of fear of social disapproval. But such needs will come out in some other manner, because they are too strong to be completely ignored. In Wright's story, Maybelle Eva Houseman refuses to come to terms with her sexual needs in a socially approved manner, but instead tries to use her racial advantage over a black janitor to force him to meet such needs. His own repressed hatred of whites is triggered by this confrontation, resulting in her death. In a more liberated society, Freud would argue, the repression would not have been required, because the two could have dealt openly with their needs, and, presumably, in a psychologically healthy society, there would not be any racism anyway.

8

Lawd Today!
(1963, 1991)

Although *Lawd Today!* was published posthumously in 1963 (the uncensored version in 1991), it was written in the 1930s, while Wright lived in Chicago. As an apprentice novel, it shows signs of inexperience, but it does anticipate *Native Son* and it is worth reading in its own right, because it is a convincing depiction of black urban culture. It conveys strong impressions of daily life for a black workingman in Chicago in 1937. The popular tunes, the movies, the language, the advertisements, the street vendors, the political propaganda—all are carefully and accurately noted by Wright's narrator. The title was a popular folk expression in the black community in the 1930s indicating exasperation with life's daily contingencies. While Jake Jackson, the protagonist, is no Bigger Thomas, he is in comparable circumstances: he has a low-paying job and has a gang of equally worthless friends; he lives on the South Side of Chicago; he despises black women and he resorts to violence. But he is much more accepting of the world than Bigger is, much more willing to justify it to himself. He is much more typical than either Bigger Thomas or Richard Wright.

PLOT DEVELOPMENT

The plot of *Lawd Today!* is based on an hour-by-hour recounting of one day (February 12, 1937) in the aimless life of the protagonist, Jake

Jackson. The date of these events, Abraham Lincoln's birthday, establishes an ironic counterpoint to the story by juxtaposing frequent quota-
tions from Lincoln's speeches and frequent reports from Civil War
battlefields with the empty, trivial incidents of Jake's life; the implication
of the contrast between the historical significance of Lincoln's birthday
and the utter lack of significance in a day in the life of Jake Jackson is that
he is a still a slave, even though 72 years have elapsed since the Civil
War ended with the legal abolition of slavery. Sadly, Jake is totally unaware of this ironic contrast between his life and the Civil War period, or
at least it seems to be Wright's intention to portray this ignorance in
Jake. (If one considers that from the point of view of the white South,
however, the South won the Civil War—for in some ways, blacks were
worse off after the war than before it—then Wright's intended structural
irony does not obtain.)

Part One, "Commonplace," begins at 8 A.M. with the narrator telling
us of a dream Jake is having about climbing steps that never end, a night-
mare that recalls Sisyphus's fate in Greek mythology: Sisyphus was required to roll a rock up a hill over and over again, for it inevitably rolled
down every time it approached the top of the hill. But there is no top to
Jake's stairs, so he will not even have the luxury of intervals of going
down the steps to start the climb again. Rousing himself from his dream,
Jake yells at his unfortunate wife, Lil, to close the door so he will not hear
the radio anymore, but he is unable to get back to sleep when his head
hits the hard edge of a magazine titled *Unity*, which belongs to Lil and
which is "devoted to Christian healing" (7). Jake hurls it across the bedroom, wondering why his wife keeps such "trash" in bed.

Preparing to shave, Jake overhears Lil talking to the milkman, which
makes him still more irritable. What he cannot understand—why his
wife would want to talk to the milkman—is clear to the reader: any diversion from her husband is a relief to Lil, who fears and detests her brut-
ish spouse. Because she has just had an abortion, Lil could not be having
an affair with the milkman, but Jake discounts that, instead insisting to
Lil that she is "no good" (12) to him, that she is "just one more no good
woman" (12). In this same painful conversation, we learn that Jake
tricked Lil into having the abortion by a quack doctor. Wright depicts a
number of unhappy marriages in his work, but this one may be the hard-
est to bear. In an effort to provoke Jake, Lil tells him that the doctor not
only expects payment for the abortion, but he also plans to operate on

Lil for a tumor. Jake worries that if he does not pay the doctor, Lil will complain to his employer, the United States Post Office. Because she has already lodged two complaints, Jake fears that a third one could get him fired. The pressure of the confrontation builds until, after accusing Lil of deceiving him into marrying her by falsely claiming to be pregnant, he assaults her: "Jake's open palm caught her square on her cheek, sounding like a pistol shot. She spun around from the force of the blow, falling weakly against the wall, screaming" (17). After slapping her again, he kicks her in the side. He then threatens more violence unless she puts breakfast on the table, and yet he senses no irony whatsoever in his notion that she "was taking every ounce of joy out of his life" (19).

Finally getting down to shaving, Jake takes a painfully long time in calculating how long it will take him to repay a $1,000 medical bill at $5 a month. After taking a bath while he sings some songs that were popular in the 1930s, he launches a military-like attack on his hair, which ends in a temporary victory: "The battle waxed furious. The comb suffered heavy losses, and fell back slowly. One by one teeth snapped until they littered the bathmat and washbowl" (24). After spending an inordinate amount of time selecting which of his ten suits to wear, Jake sits down to breakfast and gets Lil to fetch his morning paper, the headlines of which cause him to engage in a harangue condemning the Democrats and celebrating Republicans and money, as well as Germans and the federal government. Again, he is completely oblivious to the irony in his approval of a story about Hitler encouraging anti-Semitism. Scoffing at Communists and Bolsheviks, whom he refers to as "Commoonists" and "Bolshehicks" (33), Jake wonders why they "don't stay in their own country if they don't like the good old USA?" (33). And yet he hesitates to accept the fact that whites have recently burned a black man alive. After indulging in some sexual daydreams, he checks his mailbox, where he finds advertisements for winning the numbers and fighting impotency, not to mention "Virgin Mary's Neverfail Herb and Root Tonic for Nervous and Rundown Women."

The plot then turns toward Jake's morning routine as he kills time before his job as a clerk at the post office begins at 12:30 P.M. He visits Doc Higgins's Tonsorial Palace, where he witnesses an argument between Doc and a character named Duke. Doc and Jake ridicule Duke, who, as a black Communist, could well be someone they should take more seriously, since the Communist Party was trying to help the black community during the 1930s. (Recall that Wright was himself a member of the Communist Party when he wrote *Lawd Today!*) For $75, Doc agrees to put in a word with the postmaster so Jake can keep his job in the event that Lil reports him to his boss for slapping her. As Doc cuts Jake's hair, we hear Lincoln's first inaugural address quoted on the radio.

By now, it is 9:00 A.M. on a typical day in the life of Jake Jackson. After musing on the dangers of too much reading, Jake visits his friend Bob, who has a venereal disease. Jake's two other pals, Slim and Al, show up at Bob's apartment, and all four wonder if Father Divine, a popular religious figure in some black communities in the 1930s, is God. The narrator depicts their bridge playing hand by hand, with illustrations of the hands dealt. Leaving Bob's apartment for their jobs as clerks at the post office, the four men watch a Lincoln's Day parade, in which they see "a fat, black man whose flesh shook like fresh jelly upon his bones" (107), a clear allusion to Marcus Garvey, who led an organization called the Universal Negro Improvement Association, which urged African Americans to become economically independent and to return to Africa.

Part Two, "Squirrel Cage," takes place at the Chicago post office, where the four men and their fellow workers are indeed human versions of squirrels in a cage. Jake's unrelenting financial anxiety resurfaces when the narrator mentions his going to a Mr. Jones in the post office in order to borrow $100. Jake continues to worry, also, that Lil has already been to the post office board to lodge a complaint against him (which she has), which could get him fired. Appearing before the board, Jake denies that he beats his wife, and he even goes so far as to claim that she demands he buy her a fur coat and a piano (all lies). The board directs Jake to resign by the fifteenth of the month (in three days, as the events in *Lawd Today!* occur on February 12), but Doc Higgins's call to a member of the board, Mr. Swanson, saves Jake's job.

The work at the post office is overwhelmingly stultifying and depressing. The narrator makes it clear that the routinization and bureaucracy of the work could break down the strongest spirits. There is some slight return to life when Jake gets into a confrontation with an inspector over eight misthrown letters and when Al tries to talk Jake into joining the National Guard. Part Two concludes with the four postal workers talking about lynching, black men and white women, the Russian writer Aleksandr Pushkin (whom they refer to as "Pumpkin"), their first experience with sexual intercourse, and dirty pictures.

Part Three, "Rats' Alley," begins with the four men regaining some sense of vitality when they get off work. They go to Rose's, a combination whorehouse-nightclub, where Jake dances with a woman named Blanche. After they finish eating, they watch another woman dance, and then Jake discovers that he has been robbed. A scuffle ensues, during which Jake is beaten up by some thugs who work for Rose. Jake's day is epitomized by his dropping his last 85¢ in the snow, where he is unable to find it. At home, he ends his day the way he began it, by assaulting his wife. The last sentence of the novel reads, "Outside an icy wind swept around the corner of the building, whining and moaning like an idiot in a deep black pit" (219).

CHARACTER DEVELOPMENT

All the events of this novel center on Jake Jackson, a man with little to recommend him except for a certain low-level pleasure in existence. Jake engages in terrible physical and emotional abuse of his wife but shows no remorse whatsoever. He wastes money on the lottery, clothes, night-clubs, alcohol; he is a mindless Republican as well as a racist toward other minorities in the United States, such as Jews, Chinese, and Mexicans. He regards women, particularly black women, as subhuman. He is very ignorant and engages in no real thinking. And yet the reader may wonder to what extent Jake is a product of circumstances: he obviously did not choose to be a product of the highly antiblack culture in Chicago during the Depression, a culture that lynched blacks and denied them opportunities at every turn and a culture that exploited workers and people without money. In other words, if Jake cannot be justified, he can be explained. He even has contempt for an organization mentioned in *Lawd Today!* that does address his problems, the Communist Party. Both victim and victimizer, Jake really does not seem to be able to know, and therefore help from being, what he is. Wright seems to regard him as an average man who operates at a minimal level of awareness and is thus easily manipulated. Society's victims seem to victimize, Wright implies, as Jake takes out his frustrations on those who are weaker than he is. He has so little control over his life because he is ignorant of the forces that dominate it, and Wright never suggests in *Lawd Today!* that there is any likelihood that Jake will wake up. His character is a study in fecklessness and futility.

His three pals are all comparable to him, but they are also different from him in some key ways: Bob suffers from venereal disease and has a wife who is demanding alimony from him, Slim has tuberculosis and is constantly chasing women, and Al feels important because he is a sergeant in the National Guard and thinks "halfwhite" women are especially difficult to manage. The one black character in the novel who has some autonomy and influence is Doc Higgins, the owner of a barbershop and an important figure in the black community. Rather than challenge the system that oppresses him and his fellow black Americans, he understands how to use it to gain leverage over his existence. He makes the best of a bad situation, in contrast to Jake, who makes the worst out of a bad situation. The downside to Doc's strategy is that it supports the status quo.

The most victimized character of all, though, is Jake's profoundly unfortunate wife, Lil; Jake tends to blame her for all his problems, however blameless she is. Because of the abortion Jake tricked her into having, she does not have sex with him, which embitters him toward her. She insists that he support her, which raises the touchy issue of whether she values him as anything other than an economic functionary. Wright seems to be suggesting that the victimized victimize, and Lil is Jake's victim: even less powerful than he is, she is, as Zora Neale Hurston puts it in *Their Eyes Were Watching God,* "the mule of the world." Hardly more than a doormat for Jake's feet, she recalls Bessie Mears in *Native Son.*

In a sense, the main character in *Lawd Today!* is a way of life—namely, black life in the South Side of Chicago in 1937. The reader gets a keen sense of what human existence is like in such a community: what it sounds like, what people do in it, what they think about, how they dress, what they eat, how they divert themselves from daily life. Urban black culture may well be more intriguing than any of the other characters in the novel.

THEMATIC ISSUES

A number of themes inform *Lawd Today!,* particularly language, money, power, race, violence, and futility, the latter of which is probably the most striking to many readers. Jake's existence has no goal or point;

he just exists, and he is barely aware of even that. He learns nothing from a life that has overwhelmed him with its deadening routine. His response to futility is more of the same: drinking, playing the numbers, going to a whorehouse. His empty day begins and concludes in violence: he assaults his wife when he wakes up and repeats this act when he returns home very late at night. In the meantime, he is himself beaten up at Rose's by thugs who work for her. Although there are few white characters in the book, race plays a thematic role in the novel in that so much of black life is an effect of white racism: Jake has few opportunities because whites monopolize them; Jake tries to straighten his hair because, without realizing it, he has uncritically accepted a white standard of physical beauty; he listens to white radio stations because whites own them.

Lawd Today! is also a compelling illustration of a theme that dominates so much of literary discussion today, the theme of power, particularly as it has been articulated by the influential French philosopher Michel Foucault, who sees power as circulating everywhere in society; he cites prisons and hospitals as social institutions where power is especially concentrated and refers to such sites of power as panopticons (sites from which everything can be observed). In Wright's novel, the Chicago post office is such a panopticon: "For eight long hours a clerk's hands must be moving ceaselessly, to and fro, stacking the mail. At intervals a foreman makes rounds of inspection to see that all is going well. Under him works a legion of catfooted spies and stoolpigeons who snoop eternally. Along the walls are slits through which detectives peep and peer" (129). The powerless like Jake, his pals, and his wife, are under the thumb of the powerful at every turn in *Lawd Today!*

One reason for their lack of power is their lack of money, and money is another one of the novel's presiding ideas. Jake is a victim of a capitalist system that restricts the flow of money to those who already have it and denies it to those who need it most; a pervasive irony is Jake's admiration for the wealthy and his contempt for Communists. Every time he plays the lottery or borrows money, he unwittingly demonstrates the control capitalism exercises over his life.

And yet this novel is not completely dark, because there are sections when language offers Jake and his friends some relief from the horrible conditions of their existence, which is why the Russian literary critic Mikhail Bakhtin would probably have admired *Lawd Today!* He theorized that language can be recalibrated by the oppressed to resist linguistic control by society's dominant group. "The dozens," for example, a verbal contest in which one tries to insult one's opponent while remaining composed oneself, is a feature of black culture that provides Jake and his friends some measure of cultural independence from whites. So when Al says to Slim, "when old Colonel James was sucking at my ma's tits I saw your little baby brother across the street watching with slobber in his mouth," and Slim replies, "I remembers when my little baby brother was watching with slobber in his mouth, your old grandma was out in the privy crying 'cause she couldn't find a corncob" (91), Wright is indicating that however oppressed the black community, whites cannot stifle its linguistic playfulness.

LITERARY DEVICES AND CRAFT

Lawd Today! is interesting as a literary experiment. It is obvious, for example, that James Joyce's famous novel of 1922, *Ulysses*, was in Wright's mind as he wrote his book. Joyce's novel is based on one day in the life of Leopold Bloom, an outsider in Ireland since he is an Irish Jew, whereas *Lawd Today!* is based on one day in the life of Jake Jackson, an African American. Other reactions to *Ulysses* might include Wright's use of interior monologue (when we read Jake's thoughts in italics), the father-son theme (Leopold Bloom mourns for his dead son while Jake tricked Lil into an abortion of what might have been his son), and the lack of mythological resonance in Jake's life (as opposed to Bloom being regarded as a modern-day Ulysses).

In his naturalistic assumptions in *Lawd Today!*, Wright looks back to Theodore Dreiser's *An American Tragedy* (1925), a novel informed by the idea that the environment, particularly the moral environment, is everything in a person's life; no one, in other words, can be anything but an effect or product of environment, as Clyde Griffiths, in Dreiser's novel, is. Certainly, Jake Jackson never rises above his background. On the other hand, like *Native Son*, *Lawd Today!* combines naturalism with modernism (a literary movement that reacted against traditional nineteenth-century literature in its emphasis on fragmentation, incoherence, symbolism, and tawdriness), as is suggested by the influence of Joyce, as well as the poet T. S. Eliot, whose modernist icon, *The Waste*

Land, provides the epigraph for Part Three of Wright's novel, which is it-self a revision of lines from a sevententh-century metaphysical poem by Andrew Marvell titled "To His Coy Mistress": "But at my back I always hear / Time's winged chariot hurrying near." Wright is pulling a natural-ist message in a modernist chariot in *Lawd Today!* The long stretches of clipped dialogue among Jake and his three pals echo passages from the works of another modernist hero, Ernest Hemingway.

HISTORICAL, SOCIAL, AND CULTURAL CONTEXT

Lawd Today! is very much a reflection of life in the United States dur-ing the Depression era of the 1930s. The little world of Jake Jackson and his friends is set in the year 1937, just two years before Hitler marched into Poland, thereby beginning World War II. A racially liberal but cau-tious president, Franklin D. Roosevelt, occupied the White House, while the country was mired in an economic disaster. Blacks were still being lynched, but they were also exploring new opportunities, such as those the Communist Party offered.

The Harlem Renaissance, a flowering in the 1920s of African Ameri-can literature and African American culture in general, was pretty much over. Wright was not sympathetic to it because he regarded it as apoliti-cal and as too accommodating to racist white beliefs. He wanted a black literature that was engaged with the gritty realities of economics and poli-tics in the 1930s, when the bohemianism of the 1920s looked irrelevant.

A FEMINIST READING

Like any other work of literature, *Lawd Today!* can be read in many different ways, but one of the most suggestive ways for a contemporary audience to read it may be from a feminist perspective, a perspective that emphasizes the humanity of a group Jake and his friends deny: black women. A feminist critic would read the novel with keen sensitivity to the assumptions made about women, especially assumptions made by men; such a critic would also watch for omissions in regard to women—for instance, whether or not women are usually depicted as passive or helpless victims, rather than as characters who have at least some agency in their relations with men. Perhaps the key question for a feminist critic would be whether or not the women in the novel are considered human beings. How much understanding is demonstrated toward women? How much empathy does the author seem to have for the women characters? *Lawd Today!* may thus complicate the view of Wright as a denigrator of black women, a view based largely on *Native Son*.

Early in *Lawd Today!*, Jake indicates that Lil is "no good" (12) to him because she is unable to engage in sexual intercourse with him; her worth to him depends on her sexual availability. This is a particularly ironic stance for Jake to take in view of the fact that he is responsible for tricking her into the abortion that renders her "worthless." Rather than judge black women as individuals, Jake sees them as a dangerous category: "Either you trick them or they'll trick you" (73), he explains to Bob, without realizing that his simpleminded binary logic is not only wrong, but also unethical. Jake sees Eves rather than actual black women; it is the old story of blaming the victim instead of looking in the mirror. The deepest irony in Jake's experience with black women is why he would want to be intimate with something he regards as excrement. While Jake regards black women as threatening inferiors, he does not want them involved with white men: "I'd like to horsewhip every black cunt who so much as *looks* at a white man" (140), he tells his friends. Al, on the other hand, has found that some women's soft spot is a craving for men to beat them (156). Again, the reader needs to ask why one would want to satisfy such a craving. It never occurs to Jake or his pals to ask how one of the most powerless groups in the United States, black women, could constitute a threat to them. Jake views black women as white men view him: as hopelessly inferior. A feminist perspective on *Lawd Today!* therefore reveals the complete lack of legitimacy to patriarchy. But the price of admitting the truth of that observation is much higher than Jake and his friends can afford, even if they could come to an awareness of it.

Bibliography

For a comprehensive list of Wright's publications, readers should consult Charles T. Davis and Michel Fabre, *Richard Wright: A Primary Bibliography* (Boston: G. K. Hall, 1982). For a comprehensive list of publications about Wright, readers can consult Keneth Kinnamon, *A Richard Wright Bibliography: Fifty Years of Criticism and Commentary, 1933–1982* (Westport, CT: Greenwood Publishers, 1988). The annual bibliography in *Publications of the Modern Language Association* can be consulted for updates, as can the *Richard Wright Newsletter*. For this student companion, the American Library editions of *The Outsider, Lawd Today!*, and *Uncle Tom's Children* were used. The convenient Harper paperback editions of *Native Son, Black Boy*, and *Eight Men* were also used.

WORKS BY RICHARD WRIGHT

AUTOBIOGRAPHY

American Hunger. New York: Harper, 1977.
Black Boy. New York: Harper, 1945 (expurgated), 1991 (unexpurgated) [Harper, 1998].

FICTION

Eight Men. Cleveland and New York: World Publishing Co., 1961 [Harper, 1995].

Lawd Today! New York: Walker, 1963, 1991.

The Long Dream. New York: Doubleday, 1958.

Native Son. New York: Harper, 1940 (expurgated), 1991 (unexpurgated) [Harper, 1993].

The Outsider. New York: Harper, 1953 [Harper, 1993].

Rite of Passage. New York: HarperCollins, 1994.

Savage Holiday. New York: Avon, 1958 [University Press of Mississippi, 1995].

Uncle Tom's Children. New York: Harper, 1938, 1940 [Harper, 1993].

NONFICTION

Black Power. New York: Harper, 1954.

The Color Curtain. Cleveland and New York: World Publishing Co., 1956 [University Press of Mississippi, 1995].

Pagan Spain. New York: Harper, 1956 [Harper, 1995].

Twelve Million Black Voices. New York: Viking, 1941 [Thunder's Mouth Press, 1988].

White Man, Listen! New York: Doubleday, 1957.

SELECTED OTHER WORKS BY WRIGHT

Poems

"Between the World and Me." *Partisan Review* 2 (July–August 1935): 18–19.

"Hearst Headline Blues." *New Masses* 19 (May 12, 1936): 14.

"I Have Seen Black Hands." *New Masses* 11 (June 26, 1934): 16.

"Red Leaves of Red Books." *New Masses* 15 (April 1935): 6.

"A Red Love Note." *Left Front* 3 (January–February 1934): 3.

"Rest for the Weary." *Left Front* 3 (January–February 1934): 3.

"Spread Your Sunrise." *New Masses* 16 (July 2, 1935): 26.

"We of the Streets." *New Masses* 23 (April 13, 1937): 14.

Essays

"Blueprint for Negro Writing." *New Challenge* 2 (Fall 1937): 53–65. Conveniently reprinted in *The Norton Anthology of African American Literature*, ed. Henry Louis Gates Jr. and Nellie Y. McKay. New York: W. W. Norton, 1997.

"How 'Bigger' Was Born." Included in Harper editions of *Native Son*.

"I Bite the Hand That Feeds Me." *Atlantic Monthly* 155 (June 1940): 826–28.

"I Tried to Be a Communist." *Atlantic Monthly* 159 (August 1944): 61–70; (September 1944): 48–56.

Short Stories

"Superstition." *Abbott's Monthly Magazine* 2 (April 1931): 45–47, 64–66, 72–73.

WORKS ABOUT RICHARD WRIGHT

Fabre, Michel. *The Unfinished Quest of Richard Wright.* Trans. Isabel Barzun. 2nd ed. Urbana: University of Illinois Press, 1993.

Gayle, Addison. *Richard Wright: Ordeal of a Native Son.* Garden City, NY: Anchor Press/Doubleday, 1980.

Walker, Margaret. *Richard Wright: Demonic Genius.* New York: Warren Books, 1988.

Webb, Constance. *Richard Wright: A Biography.* New York: G. P. Putnam's Sons, 1968.

Williams, John A. *The Most Native of Sons.* Garden City, NY: Doubleday, 1970.

Wright, Julia. *Daughter of a Native Son.* Forthcoming.

CRITICISM (BOOKS)

Abcarian, Richard, ed. *Richard Wright's* Native Son: *A Critical Handbook.* Belmont, CA: Wadsworth Publishing Co., 1970.

Adams, Timothy Dow. *Telling Lies in Modern American Autobiography.* Chapel Hill: University of North Carolina Press, 1990.

Algeo, Ann. *The Courtroom as Forum: Homicide Trials by Dreiser, Wright, Capote, and Mailer.* New York: Peter Lang, 1995.

Avery, Evelyn Gross. *Rebels and Victims: The Fiction of Richard Wright and Bernard Malamud.* Port Washington, NY: Kennikat Press, 1979.

Baker, Houston A., Jr. *Long Black Song: Essays in Black American Literature and Culture.* Charlottesville: University Press of Virginia, 1970.

————, ed. *Twentieth Century Interpretations of* Native Son. Englewood Cliffs, NJ: Prentice-Hall, 1972.

Bloom, Harold, ed. *Bigger Thomas.* New York: Chelsea House, 1990.

————. *Richard Wright.* New York: Chelsea House, 1987.

————. *Richard Wright's* Native Son. New York: Chelsea House, 1988.

Bone, Robert A. *The Negro Novel in America.* Rev. ed. New Haven, CT:Yale University Press, 1965.

Brignano, Russell Carl. *Richard Wright: An Introduction to the Man and His Works.* Pittsburgh: University of Pittsburgh Press, 1970.

Burgum, Edwin Berry. *The Novel and the World's Dilemma.* New York: Russell and Russell, 1963.

Butler, Robert. *Native Son: The Emergence of a New Black Hero.* Boston: Twayne Publishers, 1991.

Cooke, Michael G. *Afro-American Literature in the Twentieth Century: The Achievement of Intimacy.* New Haven, CT: Yale University Press, 1984.

Fabre, Michel. *From Harlem to Paris: Black American Writers in France, 1840–1980.* Urbana, University of Illinois Press, 1991.

————. *Richard Wright: Books and Writers.* Jackson: University Press of Mississippi, 1990.

————. *The World of Richard.* Jackson: University Press of Mississippi, 1985.

Fabre, Michel, and Keneth Kinnamon, eds. *Conversations with Richard Wright.* Jackson: University Press of Mississippi, 1993.

Felgar, Robert. *Richard Wright.* Boston: Twayne Publishers, 1980.

————. *Understanding Richard Wright's* Black Boy. Westport, CT: Greenwood Press, 1998.

Fishburn, Katherine. *Richard Wright's Hero: The Faces of a Rebel-Victim.* Lanham, MD: Scarecrow Press, 1977.

Hakutani, Yoshinobu. *Richard Wright and Racial Discourse.* Columbia: University of Missouri Press, 1996.

Joyce, Joyce Ann. *Richard Wright's Art of Tragedy.* Iowa City: University of Iowa Press, 1986.

Kinnamon, Keneth. *The Emergence of Richard Wright.* Urbana: University of Illinois Press, 1972.

————, ed. *New Essays on* Native Son. New York: Cambridge University Press, 1990.

Kostelanetz, Richard. *Politics in the Afro-American Novel.* Westport, CT: Greenwood Press, 1991.

Lynch, Michael F. *Creative Revolt: A Study of Wright, Ellison, and Dostoevsky.* New York: Peter Lang, 1990.

Macksey, Richard, and Frank E. Moorer, eds. *Richard Wright: A Collection of Critical Essays.* Englewood Cliffs, NJ: Prentice-Hall, 1984.

Margolies, Edward. *The Art of Richard Wright.* Carbondale: Southern Illinois Universtiy Press,1969.

McCall, Dan. *The Example of Richard Wright.* New York: Harcourt Brace, 1969.

Miller, Eugene E. *Voice of a Native Son: The Poetics of Richard Wright.* Jackson: University Press of Mississippi, 1990.

Miller, James A., ed. *Approaches to Teaching Wright's* Native Son. New York: Modern Language Association, 1997.

Ray, David, and Robert M. Farnsworth, eds. *Richard Wright: Impressions and Perspectives.* Ann Arbor: University of Michigan Press, 1973.

Trotman, James C., ed. *Richard Wright: Myths and Realities.* New York: Garland, 1988.

CRITICISM (ARTICLES)

Adell, Sandra. "Richard Wright's *The Outsider* and the Kierkegaardian Concept of Dread." *Comparative Literature Studies* 28 (Fall 1991): 379–95.

Baldwin, James. "Alas, Poor Richard." In *Nobody Knows My Name.* New York: Dial Press, 1961.

————. "Everybody's Protest Novel." *Zero* 1 (Spring 1949): 54–58. Reprinted in *Notes of a Native Son* (New York: Dell Publishing Co., 1963).

————. "Many Thousands Gone." *Partisan Review* 18 (November–December 1951): 665–80. Reprinted in *Notes of a Native Son.*

Brown, Cecil M. "Richard Wright: Complexes and Black Writing Today." *Negro Digest* 18 (December 1968): 45–50, 78–82.

Brown, Lloyd W. "Stereotypes in Black and White: The Nature of Perception in Wright's *Native Son.*" *Black Academy Review* 1 (Fall 1970): 35–44.

Butler, Robert J. "The Function of Violence in Richard Wright's *Native Son*." *Black American Literature Forum* 20 (Spring/Summer 1986): 9–25.

Campbell, James. "The Wright Version?" *Times Literary Supplement* (December 17, 1991): 14.

CLA (College Language Association) *Journal* 12 (1969). Special Wright issue.

Cleaver, Eldridge. "Notes on a Native Son." In *Soul on Ice*. New York: McGraw-Hill, 1967.

Davis, Arthur P. "'The Outsider' as a Novel of Race." *Midwest Journal* 7 (Winter 1956): 320–26.

Dickstein, Morris. "Wright, Baldwin, Cleaver." *New Letters* 38 (1971): 117–24. Reprinted in Ray and Farnsworth, eds., *Richard Wright*.

Ellison, Ralph. "The World and the Jug." In *Shadow and Act*. New York: Random House,1964.

Emanuel, James A. "Fever and Feeling: Notes on the Imagery in *Native Son*." *Negro Digest* 18 (December 1968): 16–26.

Fabre, Michel. "The Poetry of Richard Wright." *Studies in Black Literature* 1 (Autumn 1970): 11–22.

Felgar, Robert. "The Cultural Work of Time in *Native Son*." *Notes on Mississippi Writers* 24 (July 1992): 99–103.

———. "'The Kingdom of the Beast': The Landscape of *Native Son*." *CLA Journal* 17 (March 1974): 333–37.

———. "*Native Son* and Its Readers." In Miller, ed., *Approaches to Teaching Wright's* Native Son, 67–74.

———. "*Soul on Ice* and *Native Son*." *Negro American Literature Forum* (now *Black American Literature Forum*) 8 (Fall 1974): 235.

Gibson, Donald B. "Wright's Invisible Native Son." *American Quarterly* 21 (Winter 1969): 728–38.

Grenander, M. E. "Criminal Responsibility in *Native Son* and *Knock on Any Door*." *American Literature* 49 (May 1977): 221–33.

Hill, Herbert, Horace Cayton, Arna Bontemps, Saunders Redding. "Reflections on Richard Wright: A Symposium of an Exiled Native Son." In *Anger and Beyond: The Negro Writer in the United States*, ed. Herbert Hill. New York: Harper, 1966, 196–212.

Howe, Irving. "Black Boys and Native Sons." *Dissent* 10 (Autumn 1963): 353–68.

Jeffers, Lance. "Afro-American Literature, the Conscience of Man." *Black Scholar* 2 (January 1971): 47–53.

Joyce, Joyce Anne. "Richard Wright's 'Long Black Song': A Moral Dilemma." *Mississippi Quarterly* 42 (Fall 1989): 379–86.

Miller, James A. "Bigger Thomas's Quest for Voice and Audience in Richard Wright's *Native Son*." *Callaloo* 9 (Summer 1986): 501–6.

Negro Digest (now *Black World*) 18 (December 1968). Special Wright issue.

Olney, James. "The Value of Autobiography for Comparative Studies: African vs. Western Autobiography." *Comparative Civilization Review* 2 (Spring 1979): 52–64.

Redding, J. Saunders. "The Alien Land of Richard Wright." In *Soon, One Morning: New Writing of American Negroes*, ed. Herbert Hill. New York: Knopf, 1963, 50–69.

Reilly, John M. "Richard Wright: An Essay in Bibliography." *Resources for American Literary Study* 1 (1971): 131–80.

Scott, Nathan A., Jr. "The Dark and Haunted Tower of Richard Wright." *Graduate Comment* 7 (July 1965): 93–99.

Siegel, Paul N. "The Conclusion of Richard Wright's *Native Son*." *Publications of the Modern Language Association of America* 89 (May 1974): 517–23.

Stepto, Robert B. "I Thought I Knew These People: Richard Wright and the Afro-American Literary Tradition." In *Chant of Saints*, ed. Michael S. Harper and Robert B. Stepto. Urbana: University of Illinois Press, 1979.

Studies in Black Literature 1 (Autumn 1970). Special Wright issue.

Turner, Darwin T. "*The Outsider*: Revision of an Idea." *CLA Journal* 12 (June 1969): 310–21.

Ward, Jerry W. "Richard Wright's Hunger." *Virginia Quarterly Review* 54 (1978): 148–53.

REVIEWS

Many of these reviews are available in *Richard Wright: The Critical Reception*, ed. John M. Reilly (New York: Burt Franklin and Co., 1978).

UNCLE TOM'S CHILDREN

Brown, Sterling A. "From the Inside." *The Nation* 146 (April 16, 1938): 448.

Canby, Henry Seidel. *Book-of-the-Month Club News* (May 1938).

Cowley, Malcolm. "Long Black Song." *New Republic* 194 (April 6, 1938): 280.

Cullen, Countee. *The African* 2 (April 1938).

Farrell, James T. "Lynch Patterns." *Partisan Review* 4 (May 1938): 57–58.

Hicks, Granville. "Richard Wright's Prize Novel." *New Masses* 27 (March 29, 1938): 23.

Hurston, Zora Neale. "Stories of Conflict." *Saturday Review of Literature* 17 (April 2, 1938): 32.

Locke, Alain. *Opportunity* 17 (January 1939): 8.

NATIVE SON

Brown, Sterling A. *Opportunity* 18 (June 1940): 185–86.

Canby, Henry Seidel. *Book-of-the-Month Club News* (February 1940): 2–3.

Cohn, David L. *Atlantic Monthly* 165 (May 1940): 659–61.

Cowley, Malcolm. *New Republic* 102 (March 18, 1940): 382–83.

Daiches, David. *Partisan Review* 7 (May–June 1940): 245.

Ellison, Ralph. *TAC* (Theatre Arts Committee), April 1949.

Fadiman, Clifton. *New Yorker* 16 (March 2, 1940): 52–53.

Jones, Howard Mumford. "Uneven Effect." *Boston Evening Transcript*, March 2, 1940, 1, book section.

Rascoe, Burton. *American Mercury* 50 (May 1940): 113–16.

BLACK BOY

Cayton, Horace. "Frightened Children of Frightened Parents." *Twice-a-Year* 12–13 (Spring–Summer/Fall–Winter 1945): 262–69.

Du Bois, W. E. Burghardt. "Richard Wright Looks Back." *New York Herald Tribune Weekly Book Review*, March 4, 1945, 2.

Ellison, Ralph. *Antioch Review* 5 (Summer 1945): 198–211.

Jones, Howard Mumford. *Saturday Review of Literature* 28 (March 3, 1945): 9–10.

Lewis, Sinclair. "Gentlemen, This Is Revolution." *Esquire* 23 (June 1945): 185–86.

Prescott, Orville. *New York Times*, February 28, 1945, 21.

Robeson, Mrs. Paul. *Hartford Courant*, April 1945.

Smith, Lillian. "Richard Wright Adds a Chapter to Our Bitter Chronicle." *PM*, March 4, 1945, m15.

Trilling, Lionel. "A Tragic Situation." *The Nation* 160 (April 7, 1945): 391–92.

THE OUTSIDER

Bontemps, Arna. *Saturday Review* 36 (March 28, 1953): 15–16.
Brown, Lloyd L. "Outside and Low." *Masses and Mainstream* 6 (May 1953): 62–64.
Ford, Nick Aaron. *College English* 15 (November 1953): 87–94.
Hansberry, Lorraine. *Freedom* 14 (April 1953): 7.
Ottley, Roi. "Wright Adds a New Monster to the Gallery of the Dispossessed." *Chicago Sunday Tribune Magazine of Books*, March 22, 1953, 3.
Prescott, Orville. *New York Times*, March 18, 1953, 29.
Redding, J. Saunders. *Baltimore Afro-American*, May 1953.

EIGHT MEN

Baldwin, James. *The Reporter* 24 (March 16, 1961): 52–55.
Ford, Nick Aaron. "Battle of the Books: A Critical Survey of Significant Books by and About Negroes Published in 1960." *Phylon* 22 (Second Quarter 1961): 119–20.
Howe, Irving. "Richard Wright: A Word of Farewell." *New Republic* 144 (February 13, 1961): 17–18.
Redding, Saunders. "Home Is Where the Heart Is." *New Leader* 44 (December 11, 1961): 24–25.

LAWD TODAY!

Ford, Nick Aaron. "The Fire Next Time?: A Critical Survey of Belles Lettres by and About Negroes Published in 1963." *Phylon* 25 (Second Quarter 1964): 129–30.

Index

About the Author

ROBERT FELGAR is head of the English Department at Jacksonville State University in Jacksonville, where he is Professor of English. He is author of *Richard Wright* (1980) and *Understanding Richard Wright's Black Boy* (Greenwood 1998). He has written extensively on black literature, with several articles on Wright's novel *Native Son* and numerous publications on Mississippi writers.